The Entrepreneur's Guide Series

HOW TO SELL YOUR BUSINESS FOR THE BEST PRICE

With the Least Worry

Vaughn Cox

PROBUS PUBLISHING COMPANY
Chicago, Illinois

This publication is designed to provide accurate and authoritative information in regard to the subject matter covered. It is sold with the understanding that the publisher is not engaged in rendering legal,
accounting or other professional service.

Library of Congress Cataloging-in-Publication Data Available

ISBN 1-55738-115-1

Printed in the United States of America

1   2   3   4   5   6   7   8   9   0

Additional Titles in
The Entrepreneur's Guide Series
Available from Probus Publishing

Contents

Preface

This book is about selling a business. It answers the question, "What is the best process, plan, or formula to follow when selling a business?" The process that is involved is explained in detail, step by step. The emphasis is on marketing—how to advertise and present the business, how to find interested and qualified buyers, increase buyer interest, negotiate the best deal, and end up with the highest price and most advantageous terms.

Selling a business is a complicated undertaking. Only those that have been involved in the process truly understand the effort and expertise that is required. The information in this book will provide you with the knowledge required to successfully complete the selling process.

I have attempted to create a complete, easy-to-read, and easy-to-understand guide to selling a business. As I became involved in selling businesses I began to look for published information on the subject. What little I found can be divided into two groups The first is the highly technical material written about accounting, taxes, and complex legal matters. The second is a collection of articles, books, and seminars that provide scant information about selling a business. None of these are in-depth, and many of them seem to be advertisements for the author rather than practical guides for those involved in selling a business.

I hope I have been successful in my task of creating a complete, pratical, and easy-to-understand guide to selling a business. However, my true level of success can be judged only by you, the reader and user of the information in this book.

This book is written for the owner (or owners) of a business. No individual needs to understand the selling process more or manage it more effectively than the owner. This book is also written for those involved in selling businesses as advisors or in some other capacity. How can they properly advise owners or complete the tasks that are part of the sale without a knowledge of the process? The third group for whom this book will prove valuable are buyers. In order for a buyer to be successful, he or she must achieve a rapport with the seller. What better insight can there be for a buyer than a thorough understanding of what the seller is trying to accomplish?

It is my sincere hope that the information in this book will be of help to those of you who are actually trying to sell a business. May you find a buyer with deep pockets and a generous heart.

ACKNOWLEDGMENTS

I would like to thank all those who have made this book possible, especially those who have helped me to learn the information presented in this book—all those who I have worked with and dealt with throughout my career. Without their knowledge and help, this book would not have been possible.

Special thanks goes to those that helped with the actual writing in some way. I would especially like to thank Sherie Cox, Molly McCabe, Greg Pearson, and Stan Cox.

My family has also played an important part in the development of this book. I greatly appreciate the support and help which I recieved from my wife Sherie and from my children Shannon, Angela, Elizabeth, Ethan, and Jonathan.

Section 1
The Basics of Selling a Business

Chapter 1
Selling a Business

INTRODUCTION

To successfully sell a business, the owner must have a clear understanding of the selling process. In order to meet his or her goals and needs, the owner must know the different steps that are required to sell the business and how those steps should be properly managed. He or she must know how to market the business, how to find and qualify buyers, and how to best present the company to a prospective buyer. The owner must also know how to deal with a business broker or with other mergers-and-acquisition intermediaries, the ins and outs of negotiation, and how to protect the confidentiality of the business throughout the selling process. This book answers these and many other questions about selling a business.

Regardless of who sells the business, the owner is ultimately responsible for assuring that a successful sale is completed. If the owner retains an intermediary to sell the business, he or she must properly manage the sales process. If the owner is going to sell the business without an intermediary he or she must understand the process and implement it properly.

The purpose of this book is to help a business owner get the utmost profit from the sale of the business. There are many different ways to sell a business; the methods described in this book emphasize marketing the company in an effort to locate the best buyer and obtain the highest possible price with the best possible terms.

REASONS FOR SELLING

Before a business owner can make the decision to sell, he or she must understand the motivation behind the desire to sell. The receipt of money is the end result of a sale. However, money is usually not the primary reason for selling. In order to make the proper decision the owner must understand what his or her needs really are. Identifying those needs usually requires serious introspection. Once a business owner truly understands his or her personal needs, then the sale of the business can be planned to best fulfill those needs.

Reasons for selling typically fall into four major categories: 1) emotional reasons; 2) lifestyle reasons; 3) personal economic reasons; and 4) external business reasons.

Many business owners want to sell their business because of emotional reasons. They are tired and don't want the hassle of running a business anymore. Often they have other interests and would rather spend time pursuing them. Some business owners become bored or burned out. What used to be an exciting challenge is now routine and tiring.

The second reason is changes in lifestyle. Running a business takes a lot of time and dedication. This level of commitment causes some to grow weary and desire a change. The change may include a change of residence, or perhaps seeking more free time to enjoy life. The motivation for a lifestyle change is often health-related.

Emotional and lifestyle reasons are internally generated reasons. They come from within a person. The prime motivation factor is usually not money—the owner wants or needs a major change.

The third reason is personal economics. Simply stated the owner wants or needs the cash that can be obtained by selling the business. He or she may still love running the business, but decides that it is more important to have the money than the business.

There is a general rule of thumb that can be followed when determining whether it is economical to sell, if the seller can net at least seven or eight times his or her annual compensation from the sale, then it would be a sound economic decision. The reasoning behind this rule of thumb is simple. The assumption is that the seller can generally earn between 12 and 14 percent on the proceeds from the sale when it is invested. If the net proceeds equal between seven and eight times the seller's annual compensation, then the seller will be able to maintain his or her annual compensation without having to work.

The fourth reason is external business factors. The old adage, "Buy when everyone else is selling and sell when everyone else is buying," applies to businesses just as well as it applies to real estate or the stock market. If you are in an industry that is popular or if there are many mergers and acquisitions in the industry, then you should consider selling, even if otherwise you have no desire to sell. The fact is that the marketplace may be offering a deal that, financially, is too good to turn down.

There are always certain industries that are "hot." The companies in those industries are "in demand"; therefore, buyers will pay substantially more. If a business owner is fortunate enough to have a good business in a hot industry, then the idea of selling to take advantage of the favorable external factors should be seriously considered.

Once the business owner has identified why he or she is considering selling the business, a selling plan can be developed that will best fulfill the seller's needs.

SHOULD YOU SELL THE BUSINESS?

For many business owners the most difficult part of selling a business is actually making the decision to sell. Making this decision is especially difficult for an owner who started the business and has managed it for many years. This owner has a very strong emotional attachment to the business. Many owners take several years to come to the decision that it is time to sell. Others can never sell their businesses, no matter what the circumstances—the business is just too important in their lives.

You, the business owner, have to decide if selling the business is the best thing for you. Be honest with yourself: recognize your source of motivation and manage the sale accordingly.

If you find you cannot sell—if you need the business in your life—accept that fact and deal with it accordingly. Don't succumb to the pressure to cash in and retire. You will only find at the time of the final closing that you can't do it.

Seek the advice of your family, trusted friends, and advisors. Their input can be invaluable. They can help you set goals for the future. They can help you determine whether you can reasonably achieve these goals by selling. However, always remember the ultimate decision is yours. *You* have to decide if selling the business is the best thing for you.

HOW DO I SELL MY BUSINESS?

There are many different answers to this important question, but the *correct* answer makes the difference between a successful sale that meets your needs and an unsuccessful sale that doesn't achieve your goals.

There are innumerable ways to approach the sale of a business. Some are clearly wrong, but there is no one method which is clearly best. There are several ways which will work; the one that works best will be a customized method which will take into consideration the needs of the business owner, the unique characteristics of the company, and the current industry and market environment.

You may wish to sell the company yourself, or you may turn the responsibility over to an intermediary. You may spend a lot of time and effort to aggressively market the company, or you may put an advertisement in the business section, tell a few people in the industry, and see what happens. You may give a prospective buyer a copy of your catalog and financial statements to review, or you may prepare a complete and thorough report that describes in detail the workings and strengths of the company. You may aggressively pursue as many buyers as possible, or you may relax once the first serious one comes forward. You may negotiate to get the highest price possible, or you may negotiate to get an "acceptable" price.

Selling a business is a marketing effort just like selling a house, selling soap, or selling any product. The same basic marketing principles apply. The better the business is marketed, the better the results will be.

THE EXIT PLAN

The exit plan, though a critical component of the selling plan, is frequently neglected by the seller. An exit plan is simply a plan that dictates how the owner will transfer the day-to-day activities of the business to the acquirer.

The exit plan allows for a smooth transition because it helps accomplish two important goals. The first is the management transition of the business. Passing management responsibility from the existing owner to either the new owner or to a management team is an important and often difficult task. The second goal is to formulate a plan for the seller for the future—the exit plan addresses what the seller will do after the sale is finalized.

Lack of proper planning causes many sellers to reconsider at the last minute. If the seller hasn't made adequate plans for the future, he or she won't know what to do as the time to sell draws closer. The seller may begin to think subconsciously that selling the business is not right, and may make an attempt to back out of or frustrate the sale.

GETTING THE HIGHEST PRICE FOR THE BUSINESS

Once the decision to sell the business is firm, the goal is to get the highest possible price and the best possible terms. Many factors combine to create the best deal. A brief discussion of some of the most important items is presented below.

Develop a Selling Plan

A well thought out considered selling plan is essential to the successful sale of a business. The plan should be a simple written outline. It should address the reasons for selling, the goals to be achieved by the owner through the sale, the selling methods, and strategies to be employed. It should include an exit plan for the business owner. Furthermore, specific individuals responsible for the different phases of the selling process should be identified. Lastly, the plan should include a timetable identifying the key dates in the selling process.

Follow the Plan

This advice should be obvious, but it is often neglected or overlooked. If the selling plan is properly prepared, the business owner can manage the selling process by periodically reviewing the plan and following up to make sure that the required tasks are being completed satisfactorily. A periodic review of the plan will also help the owner determine if the plan needs to be modified to deal with changing circumstances.

Use the Best Expertise Available

Selling a business is a unique and specialized task. Throughout the selling process the business owner will rely on advice and information from many different sources. Accountants, attorneys, employees, brokers, and others will be called upon to assist. In all situations, the owner should use the best assistance available. Rely on people who specialize in buy/sell transactions and, if possible, people with experience in the specific industry. The better the expertise and experience of those involved, the better the outcome.

Prepare the Business to Be Sold

Make the business as desirable to potential buyers as possible. Clean house; organize it so that it will show well. Provide accurate, up-to-date historical records. Provide adequate documentation of the company's technology, its manufacturing processes and procedures. Provide good personnel records, an organization chart, and job descriptions. Show the buyer that this is a well-organized and well-run organization.

Market the Business

Often in this book I repeat this critical fact—that to properly sell a business, the business must be aggressively marketed. Selling a business is just like selling any other product. The better the marketing job, the more successful the sale.

Search for Buyers

The key word here is *search*! One must find as many qualified, interested buyers as possible. Finding buyers is one of the most difficult tasks involved in selling a business. A great deal of creative effort must be used when searching for buyers. The services of a good intermediary can be a tremendous help here. The more interested buyers you can find, the higher the price you can receive.

Find a Synergistic Buyer

A synergistic acquisition is one in which the value of two companies, when combined together, is greater than the sum of the value of the two independent companies. A synergistic buyer will usually pay more for a business that possesses some quality which will make the acquiring company more valuable.

Present the Business in the Best Way

The best way to present a business is completely and honestly. Use a lot of detail; emphasize the company's strengths and its future potential. Identify the company's weaknesses and, if possible, show how they can be turned into strengths.

Negotiate the Right Way

The method of negotiation which consistently brings the highest price and the best terms is called the "auction method." This method structures the sales process to make the purchase much like an auction, with several buyers bidding for the business. To successfully use this method, careful planning and control of the sales process is necessary.

The auction method doesn't work all the time, but if applied successfully, it may significantly increase the purchase price of the business.

Meeting the Needs of the Buyer

The selling process by its nature is seller-oriented. One attempts to identify and meet the needs of the owner and to prepare the business for the sale. But a smart seller will take the time to identify and understand the needs of the buyer. Try to identify the goals and objectives the buyer hopes to achieve through the acquisition. Understanding the needs of the buyer will help the seller structure a transaction that will meet the needs of all parties and will increase the chances of successfully completing the sale.

IT'S NOT EASY TO SELL A BUSINESS

By now it should be apparent that selling a business is a demanding and complicated undertaking. To properly sell the business, a significant and resourceful sales effort will be required. Think of all the expertise represented by your company and its products. Think of all the time and effort that goes into selling those products. Think of all the time spent in servicing clients, making sure products are delivered on time, in the right color, quantity, and size. If this much effort is required to sell the company's products, how much effort is required to sell the *business*?

To successfully sell your business you must convince a buyer to pay you a very large sum of money. Finding people with that kind of money is not easy; convincing them to buy a business is that much harder. Think of yourself as a buyer: What amount of effort would you expend and what assurances would you want? How much would you investigate and how many different options would you examine? Consider these questions and you will begin to develop an idea about the amount of effort a buyer will expend before purchasing a business.

It not only takes effort to sell a business, it takes time. Although some businesses are sold in only a few months, others require a couple of years. On average it takes nine to twelve months from the time the business is first advertised until the deal is closed. Business owners and their advisors should not underestimate the amount of quality time and effort required to successfully sell the business.

DON'T LEAVE THE BUSINESS TOO SOON

Once the decision to sell is made, it is only natural for the business owner to slow down a bit. After all, he or she will only be involved in the business for a little while longer. Often the business owner becomes preoccupied either with selling or with what he or she will do with the time and money once the business is sold.

Once an interested buyer is found there is even more of a temptation to slow down and not devote the same amount of effort to the business. There is an inclination to assume that all will go well.

Don't make this mistake! Even though you are emotionally separating yourself from the business, the same level of effort must be maintained. If at all possible, *increase* the level of effort. If necessary, make yourself punch the time clock. There are some very good reasons to do so. One of the most common deal killers, one of the things that makes a buyer walk away, is an unexpected slowdown or decline in the company. The natural result of a reduction in the time or effort expended in the business is a decline in the efficiency and success of the business. Sales and profits will suffer. The growth of the company will slow and perhaps stop: The business may even experience a decline. The seller is then faced with the unpleasant task of telling the seller that the forecasts and projections of the company are incorrect. The sales and profits will be less than projected, perhaps even a decline from previous years. If the sale doesn't die, the price will be significantly reduced.

While you are actively selling the business you should run the business as if it weren't being sold. You should do what you would do if you were going to keep it and you wanted it to grow and be as successful as possible. Always remember that the buyer is under no obligation to buy your business. You never know how long it will take to sell—neglecting the business in the process makes it less desirable, less valuable, and harder to sell.

THE REWARD

This chapter has addressed the basics of properly marketing a business. Much of the discussion involved the time, effort, and expertise required to sell a business. You may wonder if it is really necessary to go to all this trouble. You may say that the business is simply worth whatever it is worth, and going to all this trouble to sell it isn't worth the effort. However, by properly selling your business you may receive a purchase price that is 25, 50, or even 100 percent higher than you might otherwise attain. There is no guarantee; but the odds are in favor of the business owner who aggressively and properly markets his or her company.

Chapter 2
The Selling Process

INTRODUCTION

Selling a business is not a scientific process. There are no exact methods to follow; nothing is carved in stone. The process is fluid—like a stream of water, the selling process can be moved and adjusted to meet the needs of the seller, the company, or the buyer. There are many different ways to successfully sell a business, just as there are many different ways to successfully sell any product.

The key word here is *sell*. Your purpose is not to give the business away or to shut it down, but to *sell* it to the best qualified buyer for the highest possible price with terms which meet the needs of both the buyer and the seller. A business is a complicated entity. It is a creation of the owner, along with the employees, the products and services, the industry, the customers, the community, and many other components. Selling such an entity is an involved process. To do it effectively requires much effort, hard work, and skill.

The selling process outlined below is a basic plan prepared for an owner desiring to actively market and sell a business. It is centered around the auction method of negotiating. The process is designed to achieve the highest price and best deal, and it has been used effectively to sell thousands of businesses.

The Selling Process

1. Deciding to Sell
2. Determining Value
3. Using an Intermediary?
4. Preparing the Business for Sale
5. Preparing the Sales Literature
6. Identifying Potential Buyers
7. Advertising the Business
8. Initial Buyer Contact
9. Confidentiality Agreements
10. Qualifying the Buyer
11. Negotiation
12. Facility Tours
13. More Negotiation
14. Receipt and Analysis of Offers
15. Due Diligence
16. The Purchase Agreement and Closing
17. The Transition Period

This outline describes the events that frequently occur when a company is marketed in an effort to maximize the return to the seller. There are an infinite number of variations on this process; with each individual company some steps may be deleted and others added to fit the unique circumstances of the company and its owner. However, the process, as here described, is quite complete.

Let's look at an example which clearly illustrates the difference which can be achieved when a company is properly marketed. A manufacturer of mechanical components used in industrial robots was contacted by an interested buyer, a Fortune 500 company. The buyer wanted to gain access to the robotic technology and to the manufacturer's customer base. The owners of the company were interested. Company information was exchanged. Negotiations were held. An all-cash offer was made.

The owners thought the offer was a good one. However, with so much at stake, they felt they should seek advice regarding the company's value. A mergers-and-acquisitions intermediary was retained. After some analysis it was concluded that there was a good chance of receiving a higher price. A sales process similar to the one described above was implemented. The company being sold proved to have wide appeal—many potential buyers were interested, and more than a half a dozen were serious enough to make an offer. An auction atmosphere resulted, and the company was sold at a final price 60 percent higher than the original offer.

Selling a unique product, like a company, to an informed and intelligent buyer is not an easy task. A good strategy which effectively markets a company will almost always result in more buyer interest, and in turn generate a higher price and more advantageous terms for the seller.

THE AUCTION METHOD

The auction method by which a business is sold in a competitive atmosphere with several different suitors bidding for the company, typically provides sellers with the highest possible prices for their business. Obviously, selling a business is a little more complicated than auctioning off machinery or equipment. But the principle of an auction will usually work to increase the sales price because it creates a market where more than one buyer competes for the opportunity to buy. To make the auction method work, a number of things have to be done successfully. The seller has to find two or more interested buyers. The buyers have to be impressed enough with the company that they are willing to compete for the opportunity to buy. Finally, the buyers must be willing and able to buy at the same time. If one buyer wants to buy today and the other won't be able to make a decision about buying for sixty days, you don't have an auction.

The auction method is not the only way to sell a business—in fact, it is one of the more difficult methods to use. But it is the one method that consistently produces the most successful outcome for the seller. The test of the seller's ability is whether an auction environment can be created.

THE SELLING PROCESS

Deciding to Sell

The most difficult part of the sales process for the business owner is making the decision to sell the business. The owner of a privately owned business has often been involved with the business for many years, or perhaps even decades. Putting it on the market is one of the most difficult decisions the business owner will ever make. Often it is more of an emotional decision than a financial or business decision. Because of the impact it will have on the business owner's life, it frequently takes an owner two to three years to conclude that it is time to sell.

Determining Value

The primary benefit which a seller receives from the sale of a business is monetary. Knowing the fair market value of the business is helpful to the owner. Many business owners have an independent appraisal of the business done to assist them throughout the selling process.

Chapter 8, "Value: Determining the Company's Worth," addresses the subject of fair market value. The chapter discusses how a buyer looks at value. Also included is a discussion of how to deal with a business appraiser. While the most direct benefit to the owner is money, the primary motivation in selling is usually something else. The business owner has other needs and objectives—addressing them is as important as addressing the monetary value of the business.

The owner's needs and how selling the business will satisfy them should be considered up front. Care and effort should be taken to assure that the sale will meet the owner's needs. The goals of the sale should be put in writing. Periodically throughout the sales process, the needs and goals should be reviewed. When offers are received they should be judged according to how well they satisfy those needs. If a buyer should develop cold feet, a review of the goals will often help to reassure the owner that selling the company is the best thing to do.

Using an Intermediary?

Who will sell the business? Will the owner sell it? Will an intermediary be hired? Intermediaries can be expensive. Are they worth the price, or is the seller better off without them?

An intermediary is anyone who acts as the liaison between the buyer and seller. They are often called business brokers, deal makers, acquisition consultants, or investment bankers. The intermediary is usually retained by the seller to represent the seller's interest. Occasionally a buyer will hire an intermediary, or the intermediary will represent both parties. The intermediary is usually paid on a commission basis.

Should an intermediary be used? In most circumstances, yes!

As an owner learns more about what is involved in selling a business, he or she will be surprised at the amount of expertise required. A business can be sold with or without an intermediary; however, most business owners do not possess the time, negotiating skills or technical expertise necessary to properly market a business. Those that may have the time often don't have the skills and vice versa. Chapter 3, "Assistants and Intermediaries," describes in detail the function of an intermediary, how to select one, and how they can best serve the seller.

Preparing the Business for Sale

When preparing a business for sale the first thing that comes to mind is usually maintenance: things such as sweeping the floor, painting the building, or cleaning out the storeroom. The physical presentation of the company and its facilities are important. Buyers like facilities which are neat, organized, and in good repair.

They are attracted to an operation which is effectively laid out and efficiently run. These are all important parts of preparing the business for sale.

In addition to physical facilities, company records and documentation must also be thoroughly prepared. The business world today is paper-oriented—buyers make decisions based upon financial information, policy and procedure manuals, and other documentation. Having up-to-date records, well-documented procedure manuals, an organization chart with job descriptions, and other relevant documents will help to convince a buyer that the business is well organized, well run, and will be easy to manage.

Preparing the Sales Literature

Sales literature usually consists of two main documents. The first is a short summary of the company, usually called the "company summary." In two to four pages it concisely presents the basic facts about the company. The strengths and successes of the company are emphasized.

The company summary is usually written as a "blind" document; that is, it is written in an effort to keep the identity of the company confidential. The name and location of the business are not given. The purpose of the blind document is to provide information to potential buyers without advertising to the general public that the business is for sale. The company summary is provided as a teaser to spur further buyer interest in the company. (Chapter 9 describes in detail how the company summary is written and used.)

The company summary is used in conjunction with a second document, a detailed, in-depth description of the company. It has many names, one of which is "detailed business analysis" (DBA). The DBA is provided to qualified buyers who agree to keep the document confidential. The DBA is the primary sales document. From it the buyer learns just about everything he or she needs to know about the business. This is the document which provides the information the buyer needs to make a decision. (Chapters 10 and 11 describe the DBA in detail.)

The sales literature also informs the buyer's advisors about the company. The buyer's accountants, attorneys, and other advisors who usually don't get involved in meetings or discussions until later in the process, first learn about the company from the sales literature. The more favorably the company is presented in the sales literature, the more likely the advisors will be to encourage the buyer to proceed with the purchase.

The importance of the sales literature is undeniable. Its preparation, its professionalism, detail, and thoroughness greatly enhance the seller's chances for success.

Identifying Possible Buyers

At this point in the selling process, those involved identify the most probable purchasers. *All* possible buyers—from employees, to competitors, to members of the general public—must be considered. The result of this analysis will be a list of potential buyers, which will contain the names of specific individuals or companies, as well as a general identification of potential buyer types or groups.

Advertising the Business

The next step is to contact potential buyers to determine their interest in acquiring the company. Depending on who is on the list, the method of contact will vary. Specific individuals or companies are sent an introductory letter and a copy of the company summary. Potential buyers in a specific industry may be contacted through advertisements in trade or industry publications. The general business community can be contacted through business opportunity ads in the newspaper. Qualified respondents to journal or newspaper advertisements should be sent a copy of the company summary.

Initial Buyer Contact

Sometime early in the relationship, it is advantageous to explain to the potential buyer how the seller wants the sales process to work.

The key points of the auction method need to be explained. The buyer needs to understand the timing as well as how the seller wants to deal with price, the exchange of information, and receipt and acceptance of offers.

Serious contact with a buyer usually begins a few days after the company summary is sent. Some basic information about the buyer will be obtained. It will be decided whether the buyer will receive more detailed information about the company. The buyer is informed of the existence of the detailed business analysis. The seller is willing to provide a copy on two conditions. First, the buyer needs to sign a confidentiality agreement. Second, the seller needs to qualify the buyer to determine that he or she is a willing and able buyer.

There is a third item that is applicable if the contact person is someone other than the business owner. Before the DBA is sent to a potential buyer, approval must be obtained from the business owner. Most owners know of people to whom they will not sell and to whom they do not want to give information. Having the seller's approval is even more critical when dealing with people in the industry. The information in the DBA is proprietary and could be used by others in the industry to gain an unfair competitive advantage over the company.

Confidentiality Agreements

The need for a confidentiality agreement was mentioned previously. It is important to avoid any unnecessary disruption of the day-to-day operations of the business. If word gets out that the business is for sale, the owner may have to spend considerable and valuable time dealing with the problems that could arise. These commonly involve the areas of employee morale, customer relations, and competitors.

When employees learn that the company is for sale, there are immediate concerns about job security. Everyone knows people who have lost their jobs as a result of an acquisition. Even if the owner provides assurances that jobs are secure, the doubts remain. There is also concern and apprehension associated with having to deal with a new management team after the company is sold.

Customers who hear that the company is for sale may become concerned about what their relationship with the new owner will be like. Will products still be available? Will they cost more? Will the quality and service be the same? Will the customer be dealing with the same people? As a result of these concerns, the customer may begin to look for other vendors. An additional concern with customers is in the area of collections. As customers, especially those with financial difficulties, learn that the business is for sale, they will pose more complicated collection problems. They will be less likely to pay their bills, or they will pay their bills slower than in the past.

Aggressive competitors always present a challenge to a business owner. However, when the sale of a business becomes public knowledge, the challenge becomes increasingly difficult. Open season is declared on all of the company's customers. Extra sales effort will be expended to lure away all of the firm's customers. Such aggressive sales efforts, combined with the customer's own concerns, can result in the loss of important customers.

For these reasons it is recommended that the sale of the business be kept confidential. It is best to announce a deal only after it is final. The seller and the buyer can then make a joint announcement to all concerned. The concerns of the employees and customers can be handled and addressed immediately. Everyone will know who they will be dealing with, and the damage caused by rumors will be minimized.

Qualifying the Buyer

When dealing with potential buyers, make sure you deal with people who are trustworthy, and who have the means and ability to buy the business and operate it successfully.

In the initial conversations with every interested party, ask about the experience, background, and financial capabilities of the buyer. As discussions progress, ask for documented, verifiable information. Since the seller is providing the buyer with detailed information about the business, it is reasonable for the seller to request certain information from the buyer as well. The seller should seek information even when the interested buyer is another business. There are many companies that appear to be very successful that really do not have the necessary resources to acquire another company.

Also ask for banking, personal, and business references. As negotiations begin to intensify, contact the references. Obtain assurances that the buyer is suitable: don't work for months on a deal only to finally discover that the buyer isn't qualified to buy.

Negotiation

Every time you talk with or meet with a buyer, you are negotiating. At this point in the selling process the conversation is almost always informational in nature. The buyer wants to know specific facts and figures about the seller and the company. Do your best to fully and honestly answer all legitimate questions asked by a buyer.

Facility Tours

Tours of the company's facilities should be given after the DBA has been distributed and reviewed and after the buyer's questions have been addressed. The tour is much more impressive and beneficial if given after the buyer already has a good understanding of the company. The facilities should be prepared for the tour. They should be clean, organized, and in good repair. (The preparation of facilities is discussed in Chapter 7.)

If possible, have all the interested buyers tour the facility within a relatively short time period. This makes it easier to keep the facility in good shape. It also keeps the buyers on a close schedule. If the facility tours are limited to a two-week period, the buyers will be forced by the schedule to be at about the same point in the buying process. This is important to the timing necessary for the auction method to work.

More Negotiation

After the facility tours, it is time to finish up the informational exchanges, analysis, and negotiations. It is important to meet with potential buyers and address their questions or concerns about the facility. Address all other questions or concerns which the buyers have, and finally request that the buyer make an offer.

Buyers are made aware of the procedure and timing of the sales process during the initial contact. They are also reminded of the process periodically during other discussions. If a buyer is seriously considering the transaction, he or she should be about ready to make an offer.

Assure buyers that you are willing to answer questions, provide information, or do anything possible to assist. Make it easy for buyers to make offers.

Receipt and Analysis of Offers

Potential buyers have been identified and contacted, information exchanged and analyzed. Interested buyers have seen the facility. Considerable time has been spent in meetings and on the telephone. All of the buyers' questions which can be answered have been answered. It is now time to receive offers.

Each of the offers should be in writing, and should be written in such a way that when approved and signed by the seller the offer will become a binding agreement on both parties.

If the auction sales method has worked, more than one offer will be received. The seller, with his or her advisors, must now analyze the offers to determine which one best meets the seller's needs. (This part of the process is discussed in detail in Chapters 16, 17, and 18.)

Due Diligence

Due diligence describes the buyer's separate and independent analysis of the company's facility and records. After an offer has been accepted, the buyer will visit the company with his or her advisors. They will examine the books and records and other aspects of the business.

There are two purposes in performing the due diligence analysis. The first is to verify that all the information provided in the DBA, during the facility tour and in various meetings, is true and accurate. The second purpose is to try to determine if the company has any "skeletons in the closet." If the buyer finds either inaccuracies in the information or "skeletons," the successful completion of the transaction is suddenly in serious jeopardy.

Inaccuracies in information cause the buyer to doubt the credibility of the seller. If errors are frequent or significant, the buyer will conclude that none of the information can be trusted and may walk away from the deal. If an unknown "skeleton" is discovered, the buyer will again begin to doubt the honesty and credibility of the seller. The buyer will ask, "Why didn't the seller tell me about this?", and, "Are there other skeletons, still hidden?"

When dealing with the buyer, be honest and forthright with information at all times. If you are not, the buyer will find out what is really going on sooner or later. By manipulating information, the seller only increases the chances of failure.

The Purchase Agreement and Closing

The writing and review of the purchase agreements and the logistical aspects of the closing are the responsibility of the attorney. This is one of the times in the selling process when the attorney plays a major role.

The attorney writes, or reviews, all documents to assure that they are in accordance with the law and to verify that the seller will receive all of the entitled benefits according to the negotiated agreement.

Prior to the close, the seller and the attorney should review together in detail all of the purchase agreements. The seller should understand the agreements, particularly any warrants or covenants which the seller has an obligation to fulfill.

The Transition Period

The transition period is the time between the close and the final transfer of ownership. In some instances the ex-owner is never again involved with the company. In other cases he or she may spend months or perhaps years training or assisting the new owner.

It is reasonable for the buyer to expect to receive the help of the seller during a transition period. The transition details should be negotiated as part of the deal. The length, compensation, and degree of involvement of the seller should be specified and agreed to as part of the transaction.

Chapter 3
Assistants and Intermediaries

INTRODUCTION

No matter how a business is sold many people are likely to be called upon for assistance. Those most often involved in assisting the seller are attorneys, accountants, intermediaries such as business brokers or mergers-and-acquisition specialists, negotiators, company employees, trade association personnel, and industry experts.

All of these professionals can be enlisted by an owner. Some are expensive to use, some are not. Some will be heavily involved with most of the items associated with the sale, others will only assist in specific tasks. The extent to which these people are used varies and is at the discretion of the owner. Some owners will want to do as much as possible themselves. Concerned about the cost of selling a business, they will usually not hire an intermediary and will use the others only when absolutely necessary. Other owners will decide that they don't have the time to sell the business or that they don't want to be responsible for the details of the sale. These owners will hire people to handle as many of the details as possible.

There are many legal, tax, financial, and other complexities involved in selling a business. It is imperative that a business owner seek appropriate counsel and expert advice in these areas. Each transaction is unique. The expert advice necessary varies depending on the individual circumstances of the company, seller, and buyer. Advice must be sought from a qualified expert. Any business owner who does not seek the appropriate advice is asking for problems.

The emphasis in this chapter will be on helping the business owner understand the role and expertise of each of these different helpers. Questions such as "Who are they?," "How do they help?," "How do you find them?," "What do they cost?," "Are they worth it?," "How do you choose one?," and "How do you work with them during the sales process?," will be posed and answered. After reading this chapter the business owner should be able to decide which of these helpers are needed, and what role they will have in the sale.

DEAL MAKERS VERSUS DEAL KILLERS

A deal maker is anyone who puts forth effort and expertise to assist in the final completion of the sales transaction. A deal killer is anyone who puts forth effort and expertise to frustrate or prevent the final completion of the sales transaction. Unfortunately, many individuals who are labeled as helpers, function, often unknowingly or unintentionally, as deal killers. Many of the helpers are by nature conservative and risk-averse. It is easy for them to over-emphasize the risks of the transaction. It is almost always easier to find reasons not to complete the transaction than it is to find creative ways to make sure the transaction is successful. It is also easy to delay the finalization of a transaction, and the longer a transaction is delayed, the harder it will be to finalize.

The owner has ultimate responsibility for a successful transaction. The owner must understand the purpose and role of each helper. Frequently a helper's personality, nature, and goals, are not in sync with the owner's. The helper may not fully understand the owner's need to sell the company. The owner doesn't get paid until the transaction is completed. If the transaction does not go through the owner gets nothing. A helper who is compensated on an hourly basis may not be sensitive enough to this fact.

The owner must make sure that helpers stay within their roles and do not enlarge them, interfering elsewhere. Again: the owner must make the final decisions—the helpers advise, but the owner decides. There is a fine line between an acceptable transaction and one that is too risky; it is the owner of the business who should decide what is acceptable and what is not.

THE ATTORNEY

Rarely is a company sold without the help of an attorney. The legal documentation which is required makes the involvement of an attorney an absolute necessity. The primary functions of the attorney are to: (1) review the information about the company which is provided to interested buyers to assure that no misrepresentations are made; (2) review or write the selling documents and contracts to assure that the seller will receive those benefits which belong to the seller based on the sales agreement; and (3) make sure that the transaction is legal and that the seller is complying with all applicable laws and regulations.

In addition to these primary functions, the attorney may provide additional services. The attorney may assist in the negotiating process. The attorney may provide advise on tax matters. He or she may also provide recommendations on ways to structure the terms of the sale. The use of the attorney in these secondary functions depends on several things. If these concerns are being addressed by someone else, or if the attorney is not an expert in these areas, then he or she should not be involved. It is the owner's responsibility to select the best person for each specific task.

It is often the case that the company's general counsel is not qualified to represent the company in this situation. The laws and circumstances relating to a sale are specialized and often complicated. It is in the best interest of the owner to find an attorney who specializes in mergers and acquisitions. To find the best attorney ask for referrals from the company's general counsel, intermediaries, and other business owners who have recently sold their business.

Selecting the proper attorney is important. The attorney should have substantial expertise and experience in mergers and acquisitions, and must be affordable. When talking with prospective attorneys, ask for the names of past clients and details of transactions in which they have been retained. Contact these clients and discuss the abilities of the attorney in question.

Also discuss with attorneys the hourly cost of their services, and get an estimate of the total number of hours required. Before the attorney can provide an estimate of hours required it will be necessary for the owner to define in detail what the role of the attorney will be. It does not take long for attorneys to incur a substantial number of hours. This can be controlled somewhat by adequately defining the attorney's role and by requiring the attorney to provide a detailed estimate of the hours required to fill the role.

While controlling costs is important, don't be so obsessed with costs that the quality of service is hindered. Keep things in perspective. If part of the deal is not properly tied down, spend the time and money to pin it down. Don't risk a half a million dollars of the deal in an effort to save a few thousand dollars in legal fees.

For some transactions it is suggested that the buyer and seller use the same attorney. Don't agree to this suggestion. While using the same attorney may save some money, the rights of the seller will probably not be adequately protected. The function of the attorney is twofold: first, to assure that the transaction is done legally; and second, to protect the client's interests. If one attorney is used jointly, only the first goal can be accomplished. It is very difficult for one attorney to protect the interests of both the buyer and the seller.

THE ACCOUNTANT

As is the case with attorneys, very few, if any, companies are sold without the involvement of accountants. Given the complexity of the tax laws and the complexity of many financing techniques, the advice of a competent accountant is invaluable. The primary functions of an accountant are to: (1) provide technical advice on tax matters; (2) assess the financial condition of potential buyers; (3) interpret and advise on the financial ramifications of purchase offers; and (4) address the financial and accounting questions which the buyer has about the company.

In addition to these primary functions, the accountant may provide additional services. The accountant may assist in negotiations. He or she may also provide recommendations on ways to structure the terms of the sale. The use of the accountant in these secondary functions depends on the accountant's abilities as well as the needs of the seller.

Selecting the proper accountant is important. The accountant should have substantial expertise and experience in the tax aspects of buy/sell agreements. Often, the company's general accountant is not qualified to represent the company in this situation. The tax laws and circumstances of a sale are specialized and often complex. It is in the owner's best interest to find a tax accountant who has special expertise in mergers and acquisitions. To locate a qualified accountant, ask for referrals from the company's general accountant, intermediaries, and others who have recently sold a business. Also agree on the accountant's cost of services—discuss the hourly rate and request an estimate of the total number of hours to be billed. Accountant's fees, like attorney's fees, can be controlled somewhat by adequately defining the accountant's role and by approving a detailed estimate of the hours required to fill it.

It is common for a seller to use two accountants. The company's general accountant can handle the preparation of the company's financial data, the buyer's questions, and analysis of the buyer's financial position. The second accountant would handle the specialized tax aspects of the transaction.

Be aware that the idea of selling the company may be upsetting to the seller's accountant. There is a good chance that after the sale, the buyer will bring in his or her own accountant—a situation your accountant would surely not relish.

INTERMEDIARIES

An intermediary can be a business broker, mergers-and-acquisition consultant, dealmaker, or investment banker. The service provided by intermediaries varies. Some provide only minimal support; others assist in all phases of the sales transaction. The best intermediaries will help in all phases of the sales process. They help prepare the business to be showcased. They prepare the sales information, help identify and contact buyers, advertise the business, negotiate with buyers, show the facility, handle the receipt of offers, assist with the due diligence, and make arrangements for the closing. They usually prepare the sales documents, do the legwork and negotiating, and absorb the costs associated with the sales process.

In return for those efforts, intermediaries are paid a commission or percentage of the total sales price. Some intermediaries charge an up-front retainer fee, which is usually nonrefundable. However, it is often credited against the final commission.

The Intermediary Industry Today

The intermediary industry today can be divided into three major segments, based upon the size of the companies serviced. Intermediaries who usually handle businesses worth one million dollars or less are called *business brokers*. Intermediaries who handle businesses worth between one and twenty-five million dollars are usually called *mergers-and-acquisition consultants*. Intermediaries who handle transactions in excess of twenty-five million dollars are generally known as *investment bankers*. The titles and classifications used by intermediaries may vary, but these are the most common.

The ranges of value which separate the categories may also vary. Some business brokers may handle transactions worth two, three, or perhaps even five million dollars. Mergers-and-acquisition consultants may occasionally handle a transaction smaller than one million dollars or larger than twenty-five million dollars, and investment bankers may occasionally handle a transaction with a value of only fifteen or twenty million dollars.

Business brokers are usually small enterprises with one or more salespeople. They are frequently associated with a franchise.

They may be associated with a real estate brokerage firm. These firms are located in most cities and service the small businesses located in the general vicinity.

Mergers-and-acquisition firms are generally staffed by five people or less. They are usually found in large metropolitan areas and serve businesses in the region of the country in which they are located. There are a few national mergers-and-acquisition firms which have multiple offices and service clients nationwide.

Investment banking firms are usually located in the major regional and financial centers of the country. Frequently they are affiliated with a major bank or stock brokerage firm, and they provide services to larger companies nationwide. Most of the services they provide are related to the public financial markets.

The intermediaries industry, especially the small and medium-sized companies, is tough and competitive. Only a small percentage of intermediaries are successful on a long-term basis. Most new people entering the profession leave it within a few years.

The industry is not subject to any effective government regulation. The few states which do require licensing require only a real estate license. The industry is small and diverse, and there are no large trade organizations which provide training and certification of intermediaries. As a result there are many incompetent intermediaries among the qualified ones.

The business owner should not decide against using an intermediary just because of the nature of the industry. Good, effective intermediaries can be found. Many do have the experience and abilities necessary to effectively market a company. The key is proper selection. In no other part of the selling process is the effort and care of the owner more important than in choosing the right intermediary.

Selecting an Intermediary

Selecting the best intermediary is an involved and detailed process which requires a significant amount of time and effort. The key factors to consider are: (1) experience as an intermediary; (2) experience in the seller's industry; (3) the past success of the intermedi-

ary; (4) the intermediary's cost; and (5) the willingness of the intermediary to commit in writing to perform in a timely manner those
things which are necessary to properly market a business.

When selecting an intermediary, begin with as complete a list
of intermediaries as can be gathered. For sources, check the yellow
pages and talk with other business owners. Include in the list intermediaries who have contacted the business owner in the past.
Talk with industry experts and trade association personnel and
consult trade journals.

The next step is to contact each of the intermediaries. The initial contact will be a telephone interview. Ask the following questions, and where appropriate, request copies of relevant documents.

Experience Related Questions:

What size businesses do they normally represent?

What types of businesses do they have experience selling?

Will the intermediary provide a resume or other documentation of their relevant experience?

Does the intermediary have experience selling other businesses in the same or a similar industry?

Success Related Questions:

What past successes have they had in selling similar businesses?

What percentage of their listed businesses have actually
sold?

How long did it take to sell them?

What do they do to assist the owner in getting the best price?

Questions about Costs:

What normal commission rate do they charge?

Are there any other additional fees that they charge? If so,
what is the amount and what is it for?

What portion of the costs associated with the sale do they cover and what do they expect the owner to cover?

Request for References:

Will they provide references? If no, say thank you and hang up. If yes, ask for several references in the following areas:

Other business owners who have successfully sold their business through the intermediary. Buyers who have bought companies listed through the intermediary.

General business and personal references. Attorneys, accountants, bankers, and others who have worked with the intermediary in the past. Other business owners who currently have their business listed for sale. (They may refuse to provide this for confidentiality reasons.)

Questions about Their Methods:

What will the intermediary do to sell the business? Ask them to go into detail about advertising, buyer searches, sales literature, negotiation, and so on.

Do they have any literature that describes their services and how they go about selling a business?

Other Questions:

Will they provide you with a copy of their standard listing agreement or contract?

How do they handle complaints? What recourse does an unsatisfied client have?

The purpose of these questions is to gather the information necessary to determine which intermediary can best sell the company. After the initial telephone interviews, the business owner should be able to eliminate many of the intermediaries on the list. After the business owner has reviewed the documents provided by the different intermediaries, the list should be reduced to two or three names.

The business owner should then meet personally with the remaining intermediaries. He or she should listen to the sales presentation and review and ask questions about the intermediary's literature and documents. Review again the questions listed above. Review the selling process in detail to assure that all parties understand exactly what the intermediary will do to sell the business.

Each time the owner meets with the intermediary, the intermediary will try to get a contract signed. The contract should not be signed until the owner is satisfied with it. The business owner should talk with the references provided by the intermediary. The contract should be reviewed by the seller's attorney. It should be modified, if necessary, to include the guaranties of intermediary performance.

Substantial effort should be spent checking the references provided. Contact and talk with all of them. Ask them about their experiences with the intermediary. Ask them if they would recommend the intermediary. Ask them if they would personally use the intermediary. The references provided by the intermediary will almost surely give a good recommendation. The intermediary would probably not give you the name of an unsatisfied customer. To get a more balanced perspective, ask the references for the names of other people they know who have had dealings with the intermediary. Contact these people to get their comments on the abilities of the intermediary.

Occasionally an intermediary will refuse to provide references citing confidentiality. The intermediary will claim that the names of buyers, sellers, and listed companies must be protected. Occasionally this may be true, but usually confidentiality is not an issue after the sale has been finalized. If intermediaries refuse to give references, it is usually because they don't have any or they simply won't take the time and effort. It is recommended that a business owner not trust the sale of the business to anyone who cannot provide reputable references.

The business owner and the intermediary should agree on how the intermediary will market the company. This understanding should be in writing and attached to the brokerage agreement. Each intermediary will put forth a different level of effort. The business owner should have in writing a description of the efforts and sales techniques the intermediary plans on using. A list of some of the items that could be addressed in this document are described below.

Advertising What types of advertising will the intermediary use? How frequently will the intermediary advertise? Will the intermediary be responsible for all costs of advertising?

Buyer Search How many and what type of buyers does the intermediary have access to? What will the intermediary do to identify and contact buyers?

Buyer Screening and Qualification How will the intermediary screen and qualify interested buyers?

Business Analysis and Appraisal What services will the intermediary provide in this area? Will an appraisal of the business and/or the important assets be made? What sales literature will the intermediary create? How detailed and complete will that sales literature be?

Confidentiality Does the intermediary understand the importance of confidentiality? Will the intermediary maintain confidentiality and assure that the interested buyers also will?

Facility Tours Will the intermediary prepare and conduct *all* buyer tours of the company?

Negotiation What are the intermediary's responsibilities? Will they arrange and conduct all negotiation sessions?

Client Contact and Review How often will the intermediary review the status of the sale with the seller? Will the intermediary review the selling strategy periodically with the seller? Will selling documents, buyer lists, and such be reviewed with the seller before they are put to use?

A timetable should accompany the agreement, providing a time frame for implementing the different marketing steps. This will allow the business owner to judge how aggressively the intermediary is taking the business to market.

The Cost of an Intermediary

Most intermediaries earn their fees from two sources. The first source is the retainer fee. This fee, paid in advance by the seller, is used by the intermediary to help pay the up-front expenses related to marketing the company. The amount of the retainer fee varies based on the policy of the intermediary and the size of the company being sold.

Generally the larger the company being sold, the larger the retainer fee. While the retainer fee is nonrefundable, it is usually (but not always) credited against the commission received by the intermediary when the business is sold.

The second source of payment to an intermediary is a commission. Successful intermediaries earn most of their income through commission. The commission will be a percentage of the total sale price of the company. The percentage charged will vary based on the size of the company and the fee structure of the intermediary. Generally, the larger the company and the greater the value, the smaller the percentage.

For companies valued at less than one million dollars, most intermediaries charge a 10 percent commission. Many intermediaries have a minimum commission that they charge regardless of the final sales price of the company.

For companies valued in excess of one million dollars, various sliding scales are used. The most well known is the Lehman formula, named for the Lehman Brothers company where it was first developed and used. Under this formula, the commission rate is 5 percent of the first one million dollars plus 4 percent of the second million dollars plus 3 percent of the third million dollars plus 2 percent of the fourth million dollars plus 1 percent of all value in excess of four million dollars.

While the Lehman formula is the most widely used formula,

many intermediaries use different formulas for charging commissions. Recently commissions have tended to rise. Many intermediaries today work on a sliding scale similar to the Lehman formula, but begin with a higher percentage. Six, eight, or even ten percent on the first million is not uncommon.

It is easy to see that when a company is worth a lot of money, the fees paid to an intermediary can be very substantial. Every business owner would like to avoid this expense; in fact, many business owners sell the business themselves in an effort to do so. The appropriate question for the seller to ask is, will the intermediary be able to sell the business at a high enough price to justify the commission? Obviously, if the intermediary can get 20 percent more for the business than could be achieved through a "for sale by owner" arrangement, then a 10 percent commission is reasonable.

However, it is difficult to determine if the intermediary will be successful at getting a higher price. Sometimes they are successful and sometimes they are not. Some intermediaries are consistently more successful at getting a premium price than others—the goal of the owner is to find them.

Every intermediary has his or her own set commission rate. There are no standard rates within the industry. However, in many cases the amount of the retainer and the commission percentage can be negotiated. This is especially true if the company being sold is likely to attract a lot of buyer interest. Each business owner must make a decision about using an intermediary. It is the author's opinion that if care is taken to select the best intermediary, then the services provided are usually worth the price. Very few business owners are willing or able to make the commitment in time, effort, and expertise to sell a business. Therefore, a good intermediary will usually do a better job.

The Brokerage Agreement

Once an intermediary is selected, the brokerage agreement is negotiated and signed by both parties. This is the contract whereby the seller engages the intermediary to sell the company. The intermediary agrees to extend a reasonable effort to sell the business, and the seller agrees to pay the intermediary if and when the sale is finalized.

The agreement, or contract, can be divided into three parts. The first part defines the parties involved, the property to be sold, and the basic agreement that the intermediary will sell the business for the seller. The second part of the contract identifies the sellers obligations pertaining to the contract. Most of the obligations of the seller relate to the payment of the commission. The third part of the contract identifies the intermediary's obligations relative to the sale. The written list of the intermediary's responsibilities, previously discussed, should also be included in this section of the document.

The problem with many agreements is that the first two parts are clearly spelled out and contain adequate detail, but the third is usually very brief and very vague. It usually reads something like this: "The intermediary will make a reasonable and prudent effort to attempt to sell the business."

Most agreements are clearly lopsided. They define only the obligations of the seller. They are written to protect the rights of the intermediary. The rights of the intermediary should be protected and he or she should be compensated for a job well done, but the rights of the seller must also be addressed. The seller should be protected against an intermediary who does a poor job. The brokerage agreement must specify the responsibilities of the intermediary. The business owner should insist on this. One of the tests of competent and self-confident intermediaries is their willingness to back up their claims in a legally binding contract.

In addition to specifying the responsibilities of the intermediary, the agreement should spell out penalties for nonperformance. The seller must have recourse if the intermediary does not perform or has misrepresented his or her abilities and qualifications. At the very minimum the business owner needs to have the right to cancel the agreement.

While the issue of intermediary performance is important and must be addressed in the agreement, the seller needs to be careful not to make the contract so rigid that the intermediary has no flexibility. As previously discussed, selling a business is a flexible process. While the seller needs to have guaranties that the intermediary will perform, the intermediary needs to have enough freedom to be able to respond to marketplace situations which require changes in selling strategy.

A list of specific items that should be included in the brokerage agreement follows:

1. An exact description of the parties to the agreement.
2. The terms of the agreement.
3. The exclusivity or nonexclusivity of the agreement.
4. A confidentiality protection clause.
5. A protection clause against claims for commissions from other intermediaries.
6. Terms of cancellation of the agreement.
7. The amount of the commission.
8. What will activate payment of the commission.
9. When the commission will be paid.
10. Who is to pay the commission.
11. A definition of what portions of the purchase price the commission will and will not be paid on. (What about covenants not to compete, employment contracts, earnouts, transferred debt, and so on?)
12. Which sales, if any, will exclude payment of a commission.
13. The form of the commission payment (cash, stock, etc.).
14. A statement that the broker is not to receive any additional payment or commission from the buyer.
15. A detailed statement of what the intermediary will do to bring about the sale of the business.

Working with the Intermediary

The seller should also discuss with the intermediary their relationship during the sales process. One of the most frequent seller complaints is that the intermediary does not keep them informed. Discuss with the intermediary how often the seller will receive a status report. The seller should also be informed periodically about strategic marketing decisions. This is especially true whenever there is a change in strategy. There are also several times in the sales process when a seller needs to review sales documents, buyer lists, and other important items. While the intermediary does most of the work, the seller needs to be informed and must understand and approve the major marketing decisions.

The seller should request weekly status reports from the intermediary. The report sometimes will be lengthy discussions about what has happened during the past week; other times, it will be simply a brief telephone discussion where the intermediary informs the seller that nothing of significance has happened since the previous contact. Either way, the seller has a right to know what is going on.

Many intermediaries will conduct periodic selling strategy sessions. These are meetings with the intermediary's staff and associates during which the appropriate strategy for selling the company is discussed. The meetings are held either on a regular or an as-needed basis. The topic will depend on what stage of the sales process the company is in and on what the particular needs of the company are. Early on, the topic may be who the likely buyers of the company are or what information is to be included in the sales literature. Later on in the sales process, the topic may be upcoming negotiation sessions or how to respond to some difficult buyer questions. The seller may or may not be involved in these meetings. However, the intermediary should inform the seller of the critical issues discussed and review with the seller the strategies decided on in these sessions.

Even though the intermediary has been retained to sell the business, it is the seller's company and the seller must accept responsibility for the success or failure of the sales efforts. The seller must review with the intermediary all major strategic decisions. The seller also must review all of the documents sent to a buyer. Every document the buyer receives will be included among the final purchase documents, and the seller will be required to warrant that the information they contain is true and accurate. Upfront review is the best way to accomplish this. The business owner needs to manage the sales efforts just as efficiently as he or she manages the company.

THE NEGOTIATOR

The negotiator is the individual in charge of all buyer contact. More specifically, the negotiator is the individual who sits down with the interested buyers and hammers out the price, terms, and conditions of the sale.

If an intermediary is retained, he or she will normally handle all of the negotiations. If there is no intermediary, then the negotiator could be anyone designated by the seller. It could be the seller's attorney, the accountant, some other advisor, a trusted employee, or even the business owner.

The author strongly advises the business owner against acting as the negotiator. The owner should retain some other qualified individual as a representative in the negotiations. This should be done even if the business owner is a skilled negotiator with substantial negotiating experience. The goals of the seller can best be achieved by a negotiator who is not emotionally involved with or personally attached to the business.

THE EMPLOYEES

The amount of employee involvement in the sale of a business can vary from virtual absence to complete involvement. As employees often are not aware that the business is for sale, their involvement is usually indirect. Occasionally, key employees are informed of the impending sale of the business. These employees can openly and actively assist in the sale.

The most common functions performed by employees include:

1. Preparing the facilities for display.
2. Preparing financial, organizational, and other documentation needed in the sales process.
3. Compiling data to be used in the sales literature.

4. Writing portions of the sales literature.

5. Conducting facility tours.

6. Answering a buyer's technical questions.

Because of confidentiality, it is difficult to involve employees other than indirectly. However, when preparing the business for sale, gathering information for the sales literature, or answering the buyer's technical questions, there is usually no better source than employees.

When employees question the necessity of preparing such information, they are usually told that it is necessary for the development of a business or marketing plan, or that it is needed for a banker or consultant.

TRADE ASSOCIATION PERSONNEL AND INDUSTRY EXPERTS

Members of trade associations and industry experts are excellent sources of information and in some cases are of invaluable assistance in completing a sale. At the very least these people can provide industry and market information necessary for the sales literature, and often they can provide much more.

Industry experts and trade association personnel usually know of other companies in the industry which have recently been sold, and can often direct you to information about the buyers, sellers, prices, terms, and unique circumstances of those transactions. Also, these people are often familiar with intermediaries active in the industry.

Some trade associations maintain an active list of companies within the industry which are for sale. In associations where a list is not maintained, the people frequently know of interested buyers. It is common for buyers interested in a particular industry to contact trade associations and industry experts.

In the normal course of their business, industry experts and trade association personnel come in contact with buyers and sellers in the industry. Therefore, they are excellent sources of information about buyer motivation and important selling issues and trends in the marketplace.

Chapter 4

When Not to Sell

INTRODUCTION

It is said that "timing is everything." When selling a business, timing may not be *everything*, but it is important and can significantly affect the selling price of a business. There are periods in the history and operation of a business when it is more advantageous to sell—and also when it is less advantageous to sell. Businesses are investments which can be bought and sold. Prices of businesses fluctuate according to many factors external to the company. Obviously, it is best to sell when market prices are high rather than low. If it accords with the owner's personal needs, he or she should time the sale of the business to coincide with a period when the selling prices of businesses are high.

When attempting to determine the best time to sell a business, the owner must rely on personal expertise as well as the expertise of financial and market advisors. It is usually best not to rely on an intermediary to decide when to sell. Intermediaries are salespeople who earn their livings selling businesses. They make money by convincing business owners to sell; they don't make any money by telling a business owner to wait. An intermediary can come up with many reasons why the business should be sold without delay regardless of the real market conditions. Most intermediaries rarely if ever tell a business owner that it is not a good time to sell.

The condition of the marketplace and the operating position of the company are important factors which affect the price of a company. They should be seriously considered when deciding on the timing of the sale. Remember, though, that timing is not the only issue—the personal and other needs of the business owner must also be given appropriate consideration.

The times or reasons when an owner should consider postponing the sale of the business fall into two categories. The first category includes those things which relate to the company's internal operations, things over which the company has some control. The second category relates to factors which are external to the company, those over which the company has little or no influence.

INTERNAL REASONS NOT TO SELL

There are specific characteristics which make a business less desirable to a buyer. There are times in a company's history when a buyer will not be willing to pay a premium price for the business. A business owner who is aware of these factors can time the sale of the business to avoid them.

In general, it can be said that a buyer will be less interested in a business when it is doing poorly. This statement is not completely true, however, for many buyers look specifically for companies with problems. These buyers are bargain hunters who look for companies in trouble because they can buy them at very low prices. Perhaps the initial statement should be rephrased to state, a buyer who is willing to pay a premium price for a business will be less interested in it when it is doing poorly.

Avoid selling if profits or revenue are down. Buyers prefer to see smooth growth trends. If a company's growth trend has been interrupted by a decline, a buyer will be cautious and will not be willing to pay a premium price.

Also, avoid selling, if possible, when the company is in a loss position. Buyers buy to gain access to future profits. If the company has no current profits, a buyer will significantly discount any projections of future profits.

Another time to avoid selling is when the company is expected to have a major increase in revenue or profits. If a new product line is about to be introduced, or the company is about to enter a new market area, or new cost cutting procedures are about to be implemented, postpone the sale. A buyer will never pay full value for anticipated increases. It is best to postpone the sale until after they have been achieved—sell the company near the top of a growth curve.

Buyers are also very wary of any possible legal or regulatory problems. If a company is involved in a significant lawsuit or is involved in any environmental or other regulatory disputes, they should be resolved before the business is put on the market.

EXTERNAL REASONS NOT TO SELL

Buyers, typically, prefer to buy companies with borrowed money. The easier it is to borrow money and the more money a buyer can borrow, the higher the price they will be willing to pay for a business. When interest rates are high and collateral requirements are stringent, a buyer will not be able to borrow as much and therefore will not be willing to pay as much for the business. A business owner should therefore prefer to sell when interest rates are low.

During a national economic recession, money is usually tight and there are usually fewer potential buyers. Conversely, there may be many companies that are doing poorly and are looking to sell in an effort to bail out or acquire needed capital. During a recession the market is usually a buyer's market, and those buyers are looking for bargains. They are not usually willing to pay premium prices.

This fact holds true even if the company is a "recession-proof" business. If the business is such that it does extremely well during a recession, it will still be difficult to find a buyer willing to pay premium prices. Interest rates will be high; the mindset of most buyers will be that of a bargain hunter. Even if the company is an extraordinary company, buyers will try to buy it at bargain prices. A business owner should try to avoid selling the business during a period of economic decline or recession.

Sometimes a business owner may find that the country as a whole is in an economic growth cycle but the specific region where the company operates is experiencing a regional recession. Deciding whether this is a good time to sell is a little trickier. It often depends on whether the business is a regional or national business. Buyers oriented to the regional economy will see gloom and doom, and will either not be interested in buying or will be looking for bargains. Buyers with a national economic orientation will probably be influenced more by the behavior of the national markets, but they will still be aware of the region's economic difficulties, and to some extent it will affect their desire to buy as well as the price they are willing to pay.

Another thing to consider is that certain industries may be doing poorly even though the national and regional economies are doing well. If the company to be sold is part of an industry which is doing poorly, then caution should be used. If the industry has substantial excess capacity or if many of the individual participants are not doing well, it is likely that many of the participants are either for sale or are considering it. Also, buyers will be aware of the industry's difficulties and will approach the industry with caution because of its increased risk. A buyer's market will probably result; the industry's condition makes buyers wary, while simultaneously more companies probably go on the market. Buyers, looking for bargains, will not be willing to pay for the true value of a successful firm. A business owner in such an industry should consider waiting until the industry recovers before selling.

WHEN TO SELL

The old adage, "Buy when everyone else is selling and sell when everyone else is buying," applies to businesses. Roughly translated, it means sell a business when everything is going great and buy a business when everything is going wrong.

A business owner will typically receive the highest price for the business if it is sold during a growth cycle. The seller should sell during a year when the business is having higher sales and profits than at any other time in its history, and the next year looks to be as good or better.

A business owner will receive a higher price if the business is sold during a time of low interest rates along with a great bull market on Wall Street. The price will be enhanced even more if the owner sells at a time when the industry is "hot."

Deciding when to sell and when not to sell is a very difficult decision, for two reasons. First, one never knows what tomorrow will bring. The business owner doesn't know how long the good times or the bad times will last. If interest rates are low today, they might be lower tomorrow.

The second reason why deciding when to sell is difficult is human nature. It is human nature to want to hang on when things are good and let go when things are bad. This is why everyone believes it best to sell when others are buying and buy when others are selling. But only a few really practice it.

CONSIDER THE SELLER'S NEEDS

A seller who has substantial time to prepare for the sale of his or her business can monitor the market and sell when conditions are ideal. Unfortunately, many sellers do not have this luxury. If the sale is motivated by burnout or health problems, then the seller may have no control over the timing of the sale.

As discussed previously, many sellers sell for emotional and lifestyle reasons. Money is important, but not the primary factor. A seller in this situation may be faced with the difficult decision of whether to sell when the market is less desirable or whether to wait until interest rates drop and the market is improved. The key is, what are the seller's true needs? If they are economic, then it is probably best to wait. If they are emotional or lifestyle, then perhaps it is in the seller's best interest to proceed with the sale even though the market is down.

Chapter 5

Alternatives to Selling

INTRODUCTION

Selling the business is not always the best way to meet the needs of the business owner. This may be the case when the owner enjoys the business and wants to remain involved, but needs more free time or needs to retrieve some of his or her money out of the business. There are ways for the owner to remove money from the business or free up time while still maintaining an equity interest and active involvement in the company.

An owner who wants cash, but also wants to stay involved in the business, has several options. The business can be merged with another company. The owner could bring in a partner. The company could be taken public. The business could be sold, with the owner staying on for the buyer as an employee manager. Each of these options lets the owner take all or part of his or her money out of the business while still remaining active in the company's management.

If more time for outside interests is needed, this too can be accomplished. The day-to-day management of the company can be reorganized so that the owner spends less time in the business. The owner could go into partial retirement, working only a few days a week. Perhaps the organization could be restructured so that the day-to-day management would be the responsibility of an employee manager. The owner would become an absentee owner, spending only a few days per month in the business.

Another alternative to selling which is usually not properly considered, but should be, is an orderly liquidation. Certain businesses are very difficult to sell; buyers are not willing to pay anything more than a bargain basement price. Perhaps the company is in a declining or unpopular industry. If the company has significant unencumbered assets, an orderly liquidation might provide a better return to the seller than selling the business as a going concern.

Remember, the question is, Which alternative will work for you? Some will work for one owner, but not another. Many business owners find it difficult to let others get involved in the management of the business. After being the boss, the one who calls the shots and has control, they find it difficult to let go and delegate responsibility to others. Many owners believe that they can become absentee owners, but find that they cannot really abdicate the decision making responsibility to the new manager.

When considering these alternatives, an owner should consider his or her personality and management style. Make sure the ramifications of each alternative is thoroughly understood.

MERGERS

A merger combines your company with another, usually larger, company. You are compensated for the sale, in cash, stock, or some other form. It is common to receive some stock in the acquiring company as part of the payment.

The company with which the merger is made is usually a similar type of business, but this is not always so. After the merger, the operations of your company are either totally absorbed in the other company or they are set up as a division or subsidiary. Usually you remain responsible for the operations of the division (your former company). You may even be given responsibilities over additional operations.

Merging your company into another is not that different than selling it outright. The process is the same—you still prepare selling documents, solicit buyers, negotiate, and perform due diligence. The difference is in the type of buyers solicited. Solicit only companies which would make good merger partners, organizations that would fit well with your company and your management style.

BRINGING IN A PARTNER

When you bring in a partner, you sell a portion of the equity in the business. As an established business owner considering the sale of your company, you should approach this alternative differently than if you owned a young start-up company. You consider bringing in a partner because you can retrieve a portion of your money from the company while still keeping active control and ownership of the firm. Try to find a partner who possesses not only money but also the experience and expertise to handle some of the day-to-day management of the company. This allows you to cash out a substantial amount of your equity as well as reduce the time and effort spent in the business.

Partnership can be structured in myriad ways, limited only by the creativity of the negotiating parties. They can be structured to allow you to maintain control, yield control, or have equal control. It is assumed that maintaining control of the business is the alternative most desirable to you—if it were not important, you would sell the company and work as an employee.

Even though the word "partnership" is used in this presentation, the company does not have to be *organized* as a partnership. It can legally be organized as a corporation, with each partner owning the agreed on percentage of the shares.

Partners can be active or inactive. An active partner comes to work every day, draws a salary, and participates in the day-to-day management of the company. An inactive (or silent) partner is usually a financial partner. This partner typically does not come to work every day and is not involved in the day-to-day management of the company. However, the financial partner is often involved in the strategic or long-term decisions of the company. He or she may draw a salary or may take a share of the profits. In many cases, a financial partner has loaned money to the business and takes money out of it in the form of principal and interest payments.

A partnership is frequently compared to a marriage. This may be an overstatement, but a partnership *is* a significant relationship. The relationship should be business-oriented, not social-oriented. The partners must be able to work well together. Each must bring individual yet compatible strengths to the organization.

The most important factors to consider in a working partner are the existence of reciprocal respect along with the ability to work well together within your company's environment. It is not necessary that you be friends. It *is* necessary that you trust one another, that you work co-operatively, and that you can accept and support each other's decisions.

With a silent financial partner, working well together is not as important. But it is important to have a good understanding of each party's goals and needs in relation to the business and to be sure those goals and needs are compatible. Seek an inactive partner who brings more than money to the table. An experienced businessman who can solve problems and help the business grow is invaluable.

Make sure the partnership is formalized and the proper documentation, legal and otherwise, is prepared. In addition to the normal partnership agreements, have a buy/sell agreement drawn up. Every partnership will be dissolved at some time in the future, if not by you and your partner then by your estates. Negotiating the details of this eventuality beforehand will prevent many problems. Also, be certain that the buy/sell agreement contains a right of first refusal clause that gives each partner the first option to purchase the other partner's share. Don't let your partner decide who your new partner will be. Make sure you have the option to buy back the other partnership interest.

Everyone's heard horror stories about partners who hated or stole from one another, and the problems that the partnership created for the business and for the personal lives of the partners. However, many partnerships succeed, as both partners contribute to the growth of the business. In short, partnerships do not work for all owners, but they work well for many. If you feel you can personally participate in a partnership, it might provide the opportunity to free up money or time and allow you to meet your personal goals.

GOING PUBLIC

When a company goes public its stock is sold to the public. The sale is made on a stock exchange or in the national over-the-counter (OTC) market. All or part of the company's stock may be sold. The stock being sold may be newly issued stock, stock owned by the existing owners of the company, or some combination of the two. The proceeds from newly issued company stock are company funds. The proceeds from the sale of stock owned by existing stockholders belongs to those stockholders.

One advantage of going public is that the owner can sell his or her stock for cash without giving up the management of the company. Even if the owner sells all or nearly all of his or her stock, the owner will remain in control. The existing management will remain in place unless removed by the board of directors.

There is also a level of prestige associated with being in control of a public company. Many owners take their companys public to satisfy the demands of their egos.

The real advantage of going public is gaining access to public financing markets. The company can sell stock through these markets and use the proceeds to promote the future growth and success of the company. Unlike borrowed money, equity raised on the stock market has no interest payments and never has to be repaid. New stockholders, however, do expect the future appreciation of stock prices or the receipt of dividends.

There are also disadvantages to taking the company public. First of all, it is expensive. The cost will be between 5 percent and 20 percent of the sum raised. The larger the sum raised, the lower the percentage. Once the company is public it is no longer private. The salaries, perks, and other compensation of top management become a matter of public record. There are also very specific reporting requirements. Public companies are required to file quarterly reports with the Securities and Exchange Commission. The compilation of these reports can be time-consuming and expensive.

While the existing management maintains control when a company goes public, that control is not absolute. The management must now answer to a board of directors and to the stockholders. If the business is managed with an acceptable level of confidence, the management will maintain the support of most stockholders. However, there will always be some dissatisfied stockholders to tell you how you are mismanaging the company.

Taking a company public is a specialized process, subject to very specific legal guidelines, as well as detailed regulatory and reporting requirements. An owner considering taking a company public should seek expert advice and consult a good securities attorney and investment banker.

PARTIAL RETIREMENT

An owner who chooses partial retirement will reduce the time spent in the business to about half the time currently being spent. A partially retired owner usually does not sell any of the equity in the business.

Partial retirement does not necessarily mean that you retire. Frequently your extra time is spent in other investments or business interests. You could also be absent from the company for extended periods of time for travel or other purposes.

Partial retirement is not easy. It is often more difficult than absentee ownership. It is often easier for the business owner to give up all management responsibilities than to give up half of them.

The steps involved in partial retirement are as follows:

1. Prepare a description of your current responsibilities and functions.

2. Decide which functions you will keep and which you will delegate.

3. Decide whether you will give these responsibilities to current employees or hire new employees to take care of them.

4. Hire new employees, if necessary.

5. Train people for their new responsibilities.

6. Set up the appropriate controls and supporting systems.

7. Delegate responsibilities.

8. Monitor in a predetermined, appropriate way.

Be specific when preparing the list of the job functions and responsibilities which you perform. Include how often you perform the function and how long it takes you. If necessary, keep a written log of what you do for three or four weeks before you make the list. After you have prepared this job description, identify those items which require your regular attendance on the job and those items which you would not trust to an employee. Also identify those items which you enjoy doing the most and those which you enjoy doing the least. This list prepares you for the next step, deciding which functions you will keep and which you will delegate. For each job function performed, list five items: (1) the amount of time you spend on the task; (2) how often you perform the task; (3) if you would trust an employee to perform the task; (4) whether you like or dislike the task; and (5) if the task requires your regular attendance at work.

By deciding which tasks you must keep and which you can delegate, you will be able to keep your new list of responsibilities to a reasonable length. You will know how much additional time will be required for your employees to complete the tasks you delegate. You will, perhaps, be able to structure your new job description so that you will be able to perform the tasks you most enjoy. The list will help you achieve a smooth transition which meets your personal needs.

To complete your new job description, simply list all the functions you would not trust to an employee and all the job responsibilities you enjoy the most. Now total the amount of time required to perform these functions. Your goal, once you have refined the list, should be to have a time commitment of fifteen to twenty hours per week.

On the original list, you identified which job functions would require your regular attendance at work. These are duties which make it difficult for you to be away from the business for extended periods of time. If your goal is to travel, if you desire to be able to be absent from the business for several weeks at a time, then you must delegate those duties which require regular attendance.

A decision must now be made. Who will assume the tasks you are giving up and how will those tasks be transferred? If an existing employee is to assume the responsibility, you must consider that employee's work load, as well as his or her capabilities and levels of skill. Other important factors to consider include how well the tasks fit in with the employee's current job. You also have the options of delegating the tasks among two or more employees.

If in analyzing your current responsibilities you find that you spend more than fifty hours per week at the job, you should seriously consider hiring a full-time replacement. If you are currently spending, say, fifty-five hours per week, you will be spending fifteen to twenty hours per week after the changeover. This leaves thirty-five to forty hours to be picked up—the equivalent of one new full-time person.

However, you do not have to hire a full-time manager or assistant manager to take over these responsibilities. You can promote one of your more experienced and trusted employees, and hire a lower level employee to take over his or her job. There are other options as well. You should consider any reorganization which both allows the company to continue to be successful and gives you the extra time you want.

Once you have identified the person or persons who will assume additional responsibilities, they need to be trained. Explain to them, in detail, what they are supposed to do and how they are to do it. Let them observe or assist you as you do it. Then let them perform the function with your immediate supervision. Teach them the tricks and shortcuts you have developed from your experience. If they need to communicate and deal with people outside the organization, introduce them to the appropriate parties. Give your assurance to those parties that you have confidence in your replacement and that he or she has the ability and the authority to function properly. In the future, you want these people to contact your replacement rather than you.

You will soon be spending much less time with the business and the employees. There will be less communication. Steps need to be taken to fill in the gaps that will result and to assure that you receive the information you need. You will no longer be able to talk with your employees every day. A reporting system and appropriate controls need to be established. The reporting system should consist of various written reports along with regularly scheduled meetings. They will provide the information you need to monitor the success of the business and make important decisions about the future of the company.

The controls you put into place would also help you monitor important items. You won't be around every day to monitor inventory, production, receipts, or cash balances. You may no longer be signing checks or approving purchase orders. Reasonable controls need to be established to assure that your interests and the interests of the company will be protected.

Your responsibilities have now been reduced. People have been trained and are performing their new responsibilities. The reporting system gives you all the information you need and other controls help you keep the company needs secure. No matter how frequently you appear at the company, you need only spend fifteen to twenty hours per week there. You have successfully completed a partial retirement.

A few cautions are called for. First of all, let your employees do their jobs. Monitor their work, but do it from a distance. Do not interfere unless there is a problem. Recognize that in the beginning they probably can't do as well as you; they are new at it. If you give them the proper support and let them learn, they will do well. If a customer or supplier calls you instead of your employee, explain that your employee now has special authority to provide whatever is needed. Giving up responsibility is very difficult for most business owners—doing it well takes a good plan and a lot of effort.

ABSENTEE OWNERSHIP

Absentee ownership is exactly what the phrase suggests. You own the business but are absent from its daily operations. Absentee owners are typically involved in the business just a few days per month. To change your company from an owner-operated business to an absentee-owner business, simply hire a competent manager to run it for you. The owner is involved in periodic reviews of the manager's performance and major decisions.

There are certain businesses in which absentee ownership will not work. It will not work in service businesses where the expertise of the owner is the reason for customer patronage. Absentee ownership is also impractical for small businesses that do not have substantial excess profits or are one-man operations.

In an absentee ownership situation the company must pay a salary to the manager and to the owner. If there are insufficient profits to cover the increased expense, this may not be feasible. You will be forced to either underpay the manager or underpay yourself. If you can't offer your manager enough money, you will have to settle for either an incompetent or an unhappy employee. Either could be disastrous for the company.

In order to maximize your chances of success when converting from an owner-operated to an absentee-owner business, several things must be done. These include:

1. Prepare a job description of the owner's current responsibilities and the functions of the new manager.
2. Hire a competent person.
3. Pay the new manager a fair salary. Use incentives.
4. Train the new manager.
5. Establish an adequate reporting system.
6. Establish the necessary controls.
7. Delegate.
8. Depart.

Preparing a description of what the business owner does can be very informative. It will reveal what specific areas of expertise and qualifications the new manager will need. Preparing a job description for the new manager is also important. It provides the criteria to apply when judging and comparing candidates. It gives the new manager a good description of what he or she should do. It also provides the criteria to apply when setting the goals and assessing the performance of the manager.

If you fail to hire the most competent person available, you make a serious mistake. You are trusting your most valuable asset to this individual. Management incompetence is one of the leading causes of business failure. Set a minimum level of qualification and stick to it. If a potential manager doesn't have the necessary experience, expertise, training, or qualifications, find another candidate. Be careful about promoting from within. Make sure the employee being promoted is truly qualified.

Don't allow the issue of competence to destroy your efforts. Some owners use the excuse that competent help can't be found as a reason for not making the change. This is not true. Be reasonable; don't make the requirements for the new manager so stiff that no one, not even yourself, could meet them. There are other businesses similar to yours, if competent managers can be found for them, they can be found for your business. Offer incentives for achieving important performance goals.

Don't eliminate the best candidates by not offering a fair salary. As an owner you want to be competitive without overpaying. Do some research and find out what is being paid for managers in your industry. By talking with recruiting firms, compensation consultants, competitors, and others in the industry you can learn a lot about what compensation level is fair and what you can do to make the recruiting and hiring task easier and more successful.

One good way to find out what type of managers are available and the salary necessary to hire them is to place a blind employment advertisement in the classified section of the newspaper. List the required qualifications and ask that interested parties send a resume, salary history, and salary requirements. To maintain confidentiality have these items sent to a P.O. box. By so doing you will find out how many and what kind of people would be interested in a position as manager of the company, and what salary level they desire.

Once the new manager assumes the job, provide adequate training. Make sure the new manager knows what is expected. Don't assume the new manager knows everything. Make sure he or she is taught all the systems and methods that are unique to the company. Give the new manager the benefit of your experience— the company will be run that much better. Teach the manager about unique customers, suppliers, and employees. Make sure all special arrangements and contracts are understood. Teach the new manager those things that are done to maintain a competitive edge. You will soon be turning over the business to this individual's care; any knowledge that you can impart that will make the business more successful will benefit both of you. This training time is also an important evaluation time, when you determine if the person has the ability and integrity to be the general manager of the business.

As the owner and manager of a business, you have developed methods of monitoring and controlling important items. Various documents and reports have been developed that provide the information necessary to manage the company. You collect other information verbally throughout the day or week. Once the new manager takes over, these verbal communications will be lost. A reporting system to replace this lost resource must be designed and installed, one which will furnish the information you need to monitor the business in your absence. For example, if cash balances are critical, develop a cash report which would be prepared and forwarded to you periodically. Other possible reports would be sales reports, production reports, collection reports, or financial reports. Decide what specific data you need, and have it provided on a weekly or, as is typically the case, monthly basis.

For instance, a few days into the month you would receive the package of reports for the previous month. After reviewing it you would meet with your manager and other key employees to discuss the past month's operations as well as future plans. In these meetings, management policies and major decisions are discussed. Only in unusual circumstances would you become involved more often than in these management meetings.

In addition to your reporting system, certain controls need to be put into place. Some specific goals may vary from company to company, but certain controls apply to all firms. An independent accounting firm needs to be hired, one that will periodically audit the financial operations of the company and provide audited financial statements. Levels of authority and employee/supervisor reporting relationships need to be defined. Policy manuals and systems and procedure need to be established. Whatever formal guidelines are needed to assure the continued success of the business should be put into place. Remember, as you will no longer be involved on a daily basis, controls need to be established to assure that your interests are protected.

The new manager is in place and has been trained. A reporting package which provides pertinent information has been developed. Reasonable controls and guidelines are in place. Now is the time for you to delegate the full responsibility of daily management and depart. Do not postpone this: the longer you remain, the more you undermine the authority of the new manager. Not only will the new manager's authority be challenged, but his or her enthusiasm will be eroded. Let the new manager do the job he or she has been hired to do.

Changing from an owner-operated to an absentee-owner organization is not easy. The personality of the company will change. Success requires much effort. When failure does occur, it usually can be traced to a few specific items. Almost always it is the result of omitting or not properly completing one of the eight steps previously listed. The best path to success for an absentee owner is to effectively implement and manage each of those critical steps.

ORDERLY LIQUIDATION

"Liquidation" is often considered a bad word, associated with the failure of an enterprise, but this is not necessarily the case. A forced liquidation resulting from the bankruptcy of the firm represents failure. However, the orderly liquidation of a viable going concern should not be associated with failure.

An orderly liquidation should be considered when the value of the underlying assets of the company (net of liabilities) exceeds the going concern (earnings value) value of the business.

In an orderly liquidation the individual assets of the company are sold in the most reasonable and orderly way possible, the goal being to maximize the price received for each item. Because every business is different, a well-thought-out plan needs to be developed, specifically tailored to the circumstances of the company. It is also appropriate to seek the advice of a liquidation expert. They can help you determine if liquidation is appropriate given your particular situation. If an owner can maximize the proceeds from the business through liquidation, it should be seriously considered.

The reasoning behind an orderly liquidation is simple. When a company is sold as a going concern, all of the assets are grouped together and sold as one company. With an orderly liquidation, the assets are separated and sold individually. After the sale of the individual assets the company is dissolved.

Through an orderly liquidation the owner of the company can sell off assets that are obsolete, inefficiently organized, or otherwise unproductive. The owner thereby receives as much for his or her equity as possible. The proceeds can then be invested in a more profitable venture or used for personal reasons.

When to Consider Liquidation

There are three items that contribute to value: cash flow, asset value, and synergy (discussed further in Chapter 8, "Value: Determining the Company's Worth"). Liquidation should be considered when asset value significantly exceeds cash flow value or any potential synergistic value of the company. This is often the case in companies that are capital-intensive, have had little or no profits for several years and have no reasonable expectations for better profitability in the future.

Accomplishing an Orderly Liquidation

The first key to an orderly liquidation is *order*. The liquidation needs to be done in a controlled environment, maintaining day-to-day operations in a routine manner as long as possible. The second key is *confidentiality*. The fact that the company is being liquidated needs to be kept confidential as long as possible. If the word gets out too soon, disaster could result. Customers will begin to go elsewhere. Those who owe the company money will either delay payment or refuse to pay. Everyone will want a discount on every purchase.

After the decision is made to liquidate, the internal operations of the company begin to change. Externally, however, every effort should be made to maintain the appearance of business as usual. The goal is to reduce the assets of the business as much as possible during the course of normal operations. To accomplish this the inventory is not replaced as it is sold. The company's credit terms are tightened and the company aggressively collects its accounts receivable. Obsolete, inefficient, or seldom-used equipment is quietly sold off. Employees who leave are not replaced.

Over a period of time the size of the company slowly is reduced. As the company becomes smaller, more and more assets are turned into cash. With luck—and proper planning—most of the assets of the company will be liquidated this way. Inventory, receivables, and equipment reach their lowest possible levels.

At some point in time the company will be so small that it can no longer operate or cannot operate without a loss. At this point, not before, the announcement is made that the company is going out of business. A going-out-of-business sale is held, and then the business is shut down. Assets that remain are sold off piecemeal or through an auction. In the end all the assets will have been sold off, all the debts will have been paid and the remaining cash represents the owner's proceeds from the liquidation.

Section 2
Preparing the Business for Sale

Chapter 6
What's for Sale?

The obvious answer to the question, "What's for sale?," is "The business is for sale." A business, though, is made up of a collection of many assets and liabilities. Are all of the assets for sale? What about nonoperating assets? What about personal assets? Are obsolete or excess assets to be included in the sale? The purpose of this chapter is to help the seller determine which assets should and should not be included in the sale.

It is common for a seller to reorganize the business just prior to the sale and to exclude from the sale certain assets and liabilities. Often certain debts are not transferred; rather they are settled by the seller from the proceeds of the sale. In a like manner it is common to exclude certain assets from the sale. Excluded assets are transferred to the seller or sold separately from the business.

A seller can receive value from the business in one of three ways. First, the seller receives value in the form of payments from the buyer. Second, the seller may take title to certain assets not included in the sale and keep them for his or her own personal use. Third, the seller may choose to sell, separate from the business, certain assets.

To better understand how this works, one must understand two principles. The first is that it is the goal of the seller to maximize the proceeds from the sale. The seller can often increase the proceeds if certain nonoperating, personal, or excess assets are separated from the business and sold separately.

The second principle to understand is that the buyer is actually buying a conglomeration of assets and liabilities, functioning in an organized way to produce profits, to make money for the owner of the business. The buyer buys the cash flow or earnings stream of the business.

If the company has excess or nonoperating assets that are not required to maintain earnings, the owner should consider excluding them from the sale. Usually a buyer values the company based on earnings. If the company has assets which are not contributing to the earnings, the seller will receive little or no value for them when they are included in the sale.

AUDITING THE COMPANY'S ASSETS

Before the company is taken to market, a thorough audit of its assets should be made. The steps of the audit include:

1. Compiling a complete list of all of the company's significant assets.
2. Identify each asset as either an operating asset or nonoperating asset.
3. Identify any potential excess or obsolete operating assets which may not be necessary for the future ongoing success of the company.
4. Determine the value of all nonoperating assets and excess or obsolete operating assets.
5. Decide which assets the owner would like to keep for personal use.
6. Decide which assets are to be sold off for cash, and sell them.

Compiling a list of the company's assets is the first step. The list should be comprehensive and current. It should include all assets regardless of age, condition, location, or amount of use. Frequently, assets that are not in the current depreciation schedule or in the main factory provide significant value. This list or a modification of it, will also serve as the same list that you will provide to a buyer, banker, or appraiser later on in the sales process.

Once the list is completed, divide the assets into two categories, operating and nonoperating assets. Operating assets consist of those items which are used in the ongoing operations of the company. They include machinery, equipment, furniture, vehicles, and other similar items. Nonoperating assets are those items which are not an integral part of the ongoing operations of the company. They include personal vehicles, investments, notes receivable, real estate, and other similar items.

Nonoperating assets are by definition not related to the ongoing operations and future profits of the company. As such, the list of nonoperating assets is a starting point for determining what assets should not be included in the sale.

The list of operating assets should be examined further. Assets which are used every day should be identified and marked to be included in the sale of the business. Assets which are never used and are kept in the back room or in storage should be identified. These assets will be added to the list of nonoperating assets for the seller to consider excluding from the sale.

The remaining assets on the list should be those items which are used in the business, but not on a daily basis. Whether or not these assets are necessary to the business is a judgement call. The expertise of the owner or business manager is required for this decision. It may be a good idea to maintain a work record for these items over a period of time to determine the frequency of their use and the importance of the work done with them.

The owner now has a list of all the potential assets not to be included in the sale. The list includes the nonoperating assets, the operating assets which are never used, and the operating assets which are used occasionally but are not really necessary.

By selling these assets separate from the sale of the business, the owner increases the total amount of money he or she will receive for the business.

Auditing Other Assets

The audit process described above is oriented around the tangible fixed assets of the company. While asset audits are usually ori-

ented around the fixed assets, the other assets of the company
should also be considered.

Any category of assets in which the company has a significant
investment should be considered. Inventory, accounts receivable,
and all other items should be considered. Any way the seller can
reduce the assets of the company without effecting the day-to-day
operations will increase the proceeds to the seller.

A Note to Leveraged Buy Out Candidates

Performing an asset audit is even more important to a business
owner whose company is a leveraged buy out (LBO) candidate.
The most significant opportunity for value enhancement through
an asset audit is located in those asset-intensive companies that are
often LBO candidates.

An LBO is a financing technique whereby the buyer uses the
assets of the company as collateral. All or nearly all of the purchase price is borrowed. The proceeds of the borrowing are used
to pay the seller.

What does an LBO buyer do? The LBO buyer purchases all of
the assets of a company and then reorganizes the company, often
liquidating the excess or nonoperating assets for cash. What remains is the profit-generating part of the business—the LBO buyer
has performed an asset audit and sold off the inefficient assets.

The business owner can do the same thing, selling the successful, cash-flow producing part of the firm. A seller that would do
this should significantly increase his or her total proceeds from the
sale.

TIMING

When identifying and selling off excess operating assets, timing is
important. The excess assets should be identified and eliminated
before the company is actively marketed. This is important for two
reasons. First, it will allow for a period of time for the company to
operate without these excess assets, thus proving that they were

indeed excess and the operations of the company are not hindered by their removal.

Second, the removal of excess assets must be complete before a buyer becomes involved with the business. If the seller is selling off some of the company's assets while dealing with the buyer, several questions will be raised. Is the seller gutting the company, leaving only a semblance of the former company for the buyer? Is the seller selling these assets to get needed cash? If so, maybe the seller will accept a bargain price if offered quickly. In short, few buyers will understand a seller wanting to sell off assets of a company they want to buy. It is best to complete this task before any involvement with a potential buyer.

Timing is more important with operating or business-related assets than with nonoperating or personal assets. Buyers usually understand the exclusion of "personal" cars, investments, and other such assets in the company, but they will usually not understand an inventory reduction sale or an auction of excess manufacturing equipment.

DON'T DESTROY THE BUSINESS

A tendency exists among some sellers to liquidate too much of the business. They become overzealous in their efforts to get as much cash as possible out of the company's excess assets, and consequently they sell off some of the company's essential assets. This leaves the business without sufficient assets to operate and grow.

If this occurs, potential buyers will have to make a significant investment in new assets in addition to the cost of purchasing the business. This makes the business less desirable as an acquisition candidate, and therefore less valuable.

The seller should be forthright with the buyer. Consideration should be given to whether or not removing a particular asset has the potential of hindering the company's operations or reducing its future profitability. If it does, that asset should not be sold separately—it should be retained and included in the sale of the business.

Chapter 7

Preparing the Business

Every seller must devote time and effort to preparing the business for sale. Effort taken initially, before the company is put on the market, can greatly increase its value. Preparing the business means more than scrubbing the floors and planting flowers out front. It means making the business as presentable as possible. It means doing things to make it easy for the buyer to buy.

A general rule applies to preparing the business: anything that can be done to solidify the future success of the company will increase its value to a buyer. The seller should seek to project the image that the company is an excellent business, that the owners and workers take pride in the organized, efficient, and successful operations of the company.

Those things which need to be done to prepare a business for sale vary from company to company. The owner and the owner's advisors must carefully consider this issue. This chapter presents some guidelines for sellers preparing a business for sale.

FIRST IMPRESSIONS

Readers are perhaps familiar with George Bernard Shaw's "Pygmalion"—more widely known as "My Fair Lady"—in which Professor Higgins, a speech expert, teaches Eliza Doolittle, an impoverished flower girl, how to speak and act like a Duchess. Eliza eventually succeeds in convincing everyone that she is indeed royalty.

However, during her instruction, Eliza and Professor Higgins develop a relationship akin to love. But in spite of this affection, Eliza is forced to leave the Professor, explaining to him that he knows she is a flower girl and will always treat her as such, while others recognize her as a lady and treat her as a lady. The Professor's first impression of Eliza has irrevocably determined his attitude toward her. The lesson for the seller is that there is only one chance to make a first impression, and a princess is much more desirable than a flower girl. Make every effort to be as professional, efficient, and organized as possible when dealing with a buyer.

PHYSICAL FACILITIES

Make sure all physical facilities are in order: sweep, clean, paint; organize everything. Make the company look like new. Some sellers go so far as having "white-glove" inspections before a potential buyer comes for a tour.

Many chores should be done. Make sure bathrooms are clean, well-lighted, in good repair, and free of graffiti. Have the stripes in the parking lot repainted and any cracks repaired. All of the storage areas should be neat and well-organized. Replace all broken or cracked windows. Have the maintenance crew fix any broken equipment or machinery—make sure it is all clean, well-oiled, and in good working order. Have the carpets cleaned. Replace all burnt-out light bulbs. Make sure that all office furniture is in good repair. Paint, fix, or replace items as needed. Also, if necessary, call the exterminator.

EMPLOYEES

The employees' appearance is also important to a buyer. The staff should be well-groomed and efficient. They should be busy and motivated, employees should be neat and appropriately dressed. If people in the plant wear uniforms, make sure they are relatively new, clean, and in good repair.

Also, are there certain employees the seller doesn't want around during the facility tour? If so, appropriate action should be taken.

DOCUMENTATION

In today's market, potential buyers tend to concentrate more on the documentation of a company than on the physical assets. Managers today are trained in financial analysis, business plans, operations manuals, and other documents. They look to these documents to determine the success and desirability of a company. The existence and quality of such documents is important to a buyer.

The seller should make sure that all of the company's documentation is up-to-date and well-organized. It may be necessary to create new documentation to assist in the presentation to a buyer. If this is the case, be sure that the new documentation is accurate and relevant to the operations of the company. Documents created as fluff can be readily identified by an experienced eye and cause the buyer to lose confidence in the seller. The documents a buyer may want to see include financial statements, a company operations manual or a systems and procedures manual, an organization chart, a budget or business plan, and company catalogs and sales literature.

The company should have current financial statements. Financial statements prepared monthly are preferred. These should be prepared by an independent accounting firm, and if at all possible should be audited annually.

The budget or business plan provides the buyer information as to what future the seller expects for the company. Be prepared to explain the assumptions used in the preparation of the budget and to explain any variance between the year-to-date budget and actual results. Some buyers will ask to see previous budgets to compare them against the actual operating results of the company.

The operations manual or systems and procedures manual contains guidelines for the ongoing operations of the company.

Manufacturing procedures are explained in detail. Accounting procedures are explained. Personnel policies are presented. The technology used by the company may be explained. This manual contains the nuts and bolts of the company's operations; from it, one can learn what is most important about the company's operations. The presence of a complete, up-to-date manual demonstrates the seller's commitment to the continued success of the company.

An organization chart should be prepared for the buyer. It must show all of the key company personnel, how they are organized into groups or departments, and their reporting relationships. Job descriptions of all key positions as well as resumes of current key employees should be prepared and attached to the organization chart.

Have current copies of the company's brochures, catalogs, price lists, and other sales literature available for review by the buyer.

It is also very helpful to a buyer if the seller prepares a book containing sample copies of reports which are routinely produced for management. From this book a buyer can get an excellent idea as to what information will be available to the buyer after the sale is finalized. The buyer will also use it to form opinions as to how well-organized the day-to-day operations of the company are and what improvements, if any, can be made. Be prepared to show a buyer past copies of reports that are helpful in understanding the business or measuring its success.

FINANCIAL STATEMENTS

A buyer usually relies more on the financial statements of a company than on any other document. The company's profitability and financial condition are two of the most important items considered by a buyer. Timely financial statements which show an accurate depiction of the company are imperative. Financial statements should be available on either a monthly or quarterly basis. They should show adequate detail of the company's operations. If possible, they should be prepared by an independent accountant and should be audited annually.

Through financial statement analysis the buyer will observe the operating efficiency of the company. By knowing what is important to a buyer, the seller can analyze the company and make changes to improve performance before the company is put on the market.

The two primary current asset areas which a buyer will scrutinize include accounts receivable and inventory. A buyer will calculate inventory turnover ratios and receivable collection ratios and compare these ratios against industry averages. If the company's ratios are significantly different than the industry average, questions may be asked.

A low inventory turnover ratio suggests that perhaps the company has excess, slow-moving, or obsolete inventory. A high turnover ratio suggests that either the company is very efficient in managing inventory or perhaps it does not have a large enough investment in inventory and requires additional investment.

If accounts receivable collection ratios show that collections are slower than industry averages, the buyer will question the quality of those receivables as well as the efficiency of the company's collection procedures. If collection ratios show that collections are faster than the industry average, then the company is either very efficient at collecting or its credit policies are more restrictive than the industry in general.

In addition to calculating receivables and inventory ratios, there may be other ratios which are of particular importance to the industry or the buyer. The buyer will perform a similar analysis in each area that is important to the company's success.

The seller, performing this same analysis in advance, can determine the company's status before a buyer ever sees the financial statements. Comparing the company's operating ratios to industry ratios, the seller can anticipate the buyer's questions and then adjust procedures, if necessary, to bring asset balances into line or prepare responses which explain the company's procedures and why they are effective.

Personal Items on Financial Statements

Nearly every closely held business has items on the financial statements which relate to the personal finances of the owner and are not part of the ongoing operation of the business. These items may include notes receivable, notes payable, investments, and personal items such as cars, boats, airplanes, or real estate.

It is important to remove as many of these items as possible from the financial statements. Make the financial statements strictly business—keep the personal items separate. They only muddy the waters during negotiation. This is especially important with notes payable to the owner. A buyer will not want to accept these notes as real debt, even if it is real. The buyer will either consider them as equity or ignore them altogether.

Remove personal items from the corporation and have the business either pay off the notes to the owner or replace them with notes to a third party. Removing personal items from the financial statements accomplishes two things. First, there are no items of questionable ownership (personal or business) to complicate negotiations. Second, the absence of personal items in the business will assure the buyer that the company is a professionally run, straightforward operation.

RESTRICTIONS IN EXISTING AGREEMENTS

Many contracts and agreements are entered into throughout the life of a company. Every buyer asks if these agreements are assignable to the buyer or if the buyer will have to renegotiate them. If the buyer purchases the stock of the company, then the corporation remains intact along with the contracts and agreements, and renegotiation is not necessary. However, if the buyer purchases the assets of the company, then those contracts which are not assignable will need to be renegotiated.

The seller needs to review all of the company's key contracts, especially the lease. Whether these contracts are assignable can greatly affect the sale of the company. If a contract is not assignable and can only be renegotiated at a substantial increase in cost, the company's value to a buyer will be significantly decreased.

ASSUMABLE DEBT

It is usually easier to sell a house with an assumable loan than one that is free and clear. The same is often true of a business.

It is often easier for the existing owner to borrow money than for the buyer to borrow. Because of this it is easier to sell the business if the seller has already put the debt in place. The buyer needs only to make the down payment and assume the debt.

If the company being sold is asset intensive and it is likely that asset-based financing will be used by the buyer, the seller should consider borrowing the money before the company is put on the market. It will make the business easier to sell.

When considering this alternative the seller needs to consult with the appropriate advisors to assure that this is the best alternative. The seller should also make sure that the debt can be easily assumed by a buyer.

OWNER REPLACEMENT

One of the important issues for a buyer is owner replacement. If the owner has managed the business for many years, there may be a question as to whether a suitable replacement can be found and what the role of that replacement will be.

A seller can anticipate this concern and have an answer ready for the buyer. The first step is to write a job description of the owner's position. Once it is complete, the necessary experience and qualifications for a replacement can be specified. A classified ad is subsequently written. A blind ad is taken out in an appropriate newspaper requesting resumes and salary requirements. When the buyer raises the subject of owner replacement, the seller need only explain the steps taken and offer the resumes received as a list of potential replacements.

KEEPING KEY EMPLOYEES

The retention of certain key employees is often of critical concern to a buyer. A buyer will want to assure that key employees who have made the company a success in the past will be there to help the buyer continue that success.

The change and disruption of an ownership transition often cause employees to consider leaving. Anything a seller can do to assure the buyer that key employees will remain will help finalize the transaction. One creative method which will almost always succeed in keeping key employees in place is offering them an incentive for remaining with the business for a specified period of time. This incentive usually convinces key employees to remain with the company long enough to develop a good relationship with the new owner and teach the owner much of what the employee knows about the company's successful operations.

Implementing this plan is simple. The first step is to identify those employees who are most important to the future of the company. The second step is to identify the appropriate time period or other goals necessary for the employee to contribute to the successful transition. The third step is to determine the amount and type of incentive required. Buyers are usually very receptive to this idea and will frequently agree to pay the bonuses to the key employees.

One word of caution about this idea: the buyer and seller should develop the details together. The buyer may not agree as to who the key employees are or the amount of time they need to remain. Also, don't tell the employees until the sale has been completed. If the employees are told and the sale falls through, morale could suffer.

Chapter 8

Value: Determining the Company's Worth

It is not the intent of this chapter to teach readers how to value a business. Valuing a business is a complex, difficult task. Because each business is a unique entity, a competent appraisal can be performed only by someone who is knowledgeable about the business and industry, and has training and experience in valuation methodology. This chapter presents only an overview of business valuation. The emphasis of the presentation is on how buyers value businesses and what sellers can do to help buyers best understand the value of the business.

This chapter also discusses the use of professional appraisers, whether a formal appraisal is necessary, and how to select and deal with an appraiser.

PRICE VERSUS VALUE

There is a difference between price and value. We define value as the worth of the business, in money, to a particular party. When a business is being sold, the value of the business to the seller is a particular amount. Its value to one buyer may be another amount. Its value to a second buyer may be yet another amount. Its value to an appraiser is yet another. All four individuals could be correct in their assessment of value. The differences in value result from differences of opinion regarding the company's strengths, weaknesses, historic operating success, and differing assumptions regarding its future success.

A seller can sell his or her business for a good price when a buyer is found who values the business at a much higher amount than the seller. The seller is not taking advantage of the buyer; the buyer's perception of the future of the business is simply different than the seller's.

We define price as the amount of money paid when a business changes hands. The price may or may not be related to the seller's perception of value. The key to a successful sale is finding a buyer who has a higher perception of value than the seller and negotiating so that the price paid is closer to the buyer's perception of value than the seller's perception of value.

A sales transaction can be successfully completed only when the value of the business to the buyer equals or exceeds the value of the business to the seller. If this is not the case, the sale will never be completed.

HOW A BUYER WILL VALUE THE BUSINESS

There are four basic approaches to assessing value most commonly used by potential buyers: 1) value based on synergy; 2) value based on earnings; 3) value based on assets; and 4) value based on an industry formula or rule of thumb.

Each of these methods could result in a different value for the business. We will briefly discuss each of them, their critical attributes, and how the valuation methodology is applied.

Synergistic Value

Synergy exists when the value of the seller's and the buyer's companies combined is greater than the sum of their separate value. A synergistic acquisition is one which results in both the acquiring company and the acquired company being more efficient, more profitable and more valuable than either company was prior to the acquisition. While synergy is a great buzzword used frequently in mergers and acquisitions, the reality is that only a small percentage of acquisitions are synergistic in nature. Let's look at two examples of synergistic acquisitions.

The first example involves a small, high-tech company involved in the manufacture of circuit boards. The owner of this company has developed proprietary production equipment and techniques which result in higher quality, lower cost production. Quality is substantially above industry averages and cost is substantially below industry norms. Because of these factors, this company is able to sell its services and products at prices significantly below the competition and still make above-average profits.

This company has a significant technological advantage and is a good candidate for a synergistic acquisition. A large company in the same industry would be interested in acquiring this company to gain access to its technological expertise. With this technology, the acquiring company could update its own manufacturing facilities, thereby increasing the efficiency, profitability and value of the acquiring organization. Because synergistic quality (technology) can be used to benefit the operations of the acquiring company, the combined productivity of the two organizations is much higher after the acquisition than it was before the acquisition—a synergistic acquisition.

In the second example. Company A, the acquiring company, is a manufacturer of industrial janitorial equipment used in manufacturing and warehouse applications. These products are sold through a network of company-owned branch offices. Sales are made by a direct salesforce. The profitability from the sale of these products has been substantially below expectations for several years. This is the result of high marketing costs of the company-owned branch sales offices.

Company B, the company to be acquired, is a manufacturer of a noncompetitive line of products which are used in similar manufacturing and warehouse applications.

The acquisition of Company B by Company A could be a good synergistic acquisition because Company B's product line could be sold through Company A's network of branch sales offices. The addition of the second product line, compatible with the original product line, could spread the sales and marketing costs over two product lines, thereby reducing the sales and marketing cost per product. This substantially increases the profitability of the original product line while maintaining the profitability of the acquired product line.

The addition of a compatible product line could greatly increase the efficiency of the sales and marketing organization of Company A without hurting the profitability of Company B. The combined operations of the two companies are more efficient and more profitable than the two separate operations.

Obviously, a company which is a good synergistic acquisition can be very valuable to the right buyers. A corporation which is acquiring a company for synergistic reasons is often willing to pay a premium price. The price range can be very broad; the final price paid depends to a large extent on the abilities of the negotiators on either side.

There are two ways to estimate the approximate value of a company involved in a synergistic acquisition. The first is to estimate the cost to the buyer of duplicating the synergistic quality. The second is to estimate the value of the synergistic quality to the buyer. An understanding of both methods will help determine the upper end of the value range.

The estimation of duplication costs is easily defined and understood, it is the amount the acquiring company would have to pay to create, from scratch, the synergistic quality. For instance, in the first example above, the duplication costs would be the cost to the acquiring company to perform its own research and development to develop similar technological and manufacturing advantages. Keep in mind that duplication costs include both time and expenses. The acquiring company would have to spend not only money to duplicate the technology but also the time necessary to develop the technology. The more time required, the more opportunity and profit lost.

The second way to estimate synergistic value is to determine the dollar value of the synergistic item to the acquirer. This amount is simply the value in either cost savings or additional profits which the synergistic quality would provide the buyer. In the first example above, the dollar amount of the synergistic technology is the amount of money the buyer could save with the advanced technology. In the second example, the synergistic value is the amount of the existing sales and marketing expense which would be absorbed by the new product line.

In most instances, the synergistic value to the buyer will greatly exceed the duplication costs. The negotiator representing the seller will emphasize the value of the synergistic item to the potential buyer.

To determine if your company is a potential synergistic candidate, analyze the operation in an effort to identify any competitive advantages which would be of value to a larger company in the same or a compatible industry. If the company is a synergistic candidate, then the companies to which it would provide synergy should be identified and contacted first. The initial presentation should be structured to make them aware of the synergistic advantages the acquisition of the company offers.

Earnings Value

The earnings approach to value is the most common method used in business valuation. Many different formulas, methods, and techniques fall under this category including such methods as net present value, discounted cash flow, capitalization of earnings, price/earnings ratio, and many others.

The earnings approach is most easily understood when presented as a rate of return method. The purchase of the business is an investment for the buyer and the buyer has an expected rate of return. Based on the expected rate of return and the expected future profits of the company, the business can be valued.

The purchase price is the amount of the investment; the future profit or cash flow of the business is the return which the buyer will earn on the investment. The available cash flow is defined as the cash which the business earns which is available for the buyer. The available cash flow is usually analyzed on a pretax basis, before any interest or debt payments.

The value of the business is then determined by dividing the available cash flow by the required rate of return. For example, if the available annual cash flow of the business was $650,000 and the required rate of return was 25 percent, then the value of the business would be $2,600,000. This is calculated as follows:

$650,000 / .25 = $2,600,000

The required rate of return will vary from buyer to buyer and industry to industry. Basically the more risky the business and industry are perceived to be, the higher the required rate of return. In general, size is also perceived as a contributor to risk. The smaller the business, the more risky it is. Also remember that since the cash flow is a pretax cash flow the return should also be a pretax rate of return. Required rates of return vary over a wide range. They can be as low as 10 percent or as high as 50 percent.

An additional comment should be made about available cash flow. As the buyer will be receiving the cash flow the company earns in the future, the projected future cash flow rather than the historic cash flow should be used in the calculations. Many buyers incorrectly determine value based on historic rather than future earnings.

Asset Value

A buyer will want a complete list of the assets of the company and an estimate or appraisal of their value. Usually the purpose is not to determine the value of the company, but rather to determine the amount and strength of the hard assets underlying the total business value. A business entity is a collection of assets organized to produce income. The value of the business is the ongoing stream of income it will produce. Because of this, one relies on the asset value as the total business value only when the income stream earned by the business is small relative to the company's investment in assets.

In certain industries, the value of the underlying assets is considered to be the total value of the business. These are primarily resource firms such as timber companies, mines, gas and oil companies, and real estate development firms. However, in most businesses the asset value is secondary to the earnings value.

The value of a company's assets can be defined under differing assumptions. The value definitions most often used are replacement cost—new, replacement cost—used, value in place or value in use, orderly liquidation value, and forced liquidation value. Another value of the assets which is important in acquisitions is borrowing value.

Replacement Cost—New: This is defined as the cost to replace the assets of the company with similar brand new assets. This definition is rarely used for acquisition purposes. It is inappropriate because the buyer is purchasing used rather than new assets.

Replacement Cost—Used: This is defined as the cost to replace the assets of the company with similar assets of the same age and condition as the existing assets. This definition is frequently used for acquisition purposes. It is based on the assumption that assets similar to the company's assets could be purchased on the used market.

Value in Place: Often called "value in use," this is defined as the value of the assets as part of the ongoing business entity. Substituted for "replacement cost—used" when there is not a used equipment market from which to gather information. "Value in place" is determined by taking the "replacement cost—new" of the asset and subtracting from that value a reasonable amount for the economic depreciation of the asset.

Orderly Liquidation Value: This is the value of the assets if the company were liquidated, assuming that there was adequate time to advertise and sell the assets of the business. It is not appropriate to use this definition as part of the valuation of an ongoing business concern.

Forced Liquidation Value: This is the value of the assets if the company were liquidated, assuming that the company was forced to auction its assets immediately. Adequate time is not available to advertise, find buyers, or properly market the company's assets. It is not appropriate to use this value definition as part of the valuation of an ongoing business concern.

Borrowing Value: The borrowing value of an asset is simply defined as the amount of money a lender will loan against it. This definition is important in acquisitions because the more that a buyer can borrow against an asset, the more he or she can afford to pay for the business.

Each of these values has its place and proper use. When using an asset value as a part of a total business valuation, it is best to use the "replacement cost—used" or "value in place" definition.

Industry Rules of Thumb

Several industries have common formulas or rules of thumb which provide a good estimate of value. The rules of thumb are usually expressed as a multiple of revenue, income, or capacity.

Rules of thumb can effectively develop only in industries that have many similar companies. Examples of some industries where a rule of thumb is used include movie theaters, bowling centers, gasoline service stations, hotels and motels, and insurance agencies.

Rules of thumb work because buyers know that no matter how the business was operated in the past, they can go in with their own operating formula and achieve a certain level of success. For example, in the movie theater industry the rule of thumb formula is a multiple of the number of seats. This is because the buyer knows that if he or she were to operate the theater with known operating methods they would be able to charge a certain price and attract a certain number of customers. The value of the theater therefore is based on its seating capacity and not on the success of the current owner.

Similarly for bowling centers, a multiple of the number of lanes is sometimes used. For service stations, a multiple of gallons pumped per month is used. For hotels and motels, a multiple of the number of rooms is used. To find out if rules of thumb are used in your industry talk with people who are actively involved in business sales within the industry.

No one estimating the value of a business should rely solely on a rule of thumb formula. A rule of thumb should be used in conjunction with other valuation methods. Also remember that rules of thumb are often exaggerated. In the course of casual conversation some business owners will exaggerate the value of their businesses. When you talk to people actually involved in acquisitions you will often find that the range of the multiple is really 20 percent to 25 percent less than is commonly claimed by business owners.

COST TO REPRODUCE

The "cost-to-reproduce" appraisal principle is frequently used in real estate. It is not specifically used in business valuation, but the underlying principle affects value.

Simply stated, the cost to reproduce is defined as the cost to create a similar business from scratch considering both the monetary cost and the time required.

If creating a similar business from scratch is easy and inexpensive, then there is a downward pressure on value. Regardless of the profitability or success of a business, a buyer will not pay more for the business than it would cost to create a similar business from scratch.

If creating a similar business from scratch is difficult, then there may be a value premium attached to the business. When a business is capital intensive, requires special regulatory approval, or is such that a successful operation takes a long time to develop then it is said that there are high barriers to entry. When this is the case, the business may have a premium attached to its value.

This premium is paid because the long term success of the company is believed to be more certain. Due to the high barriers to entry, increased competition from new entrants in the industry is less likely.

PRESENTATION AFFECTS PRICE

The manner in which a business is presented to a buyer affects the buyer's perception of value. The effectiveness or ineffectiveness of the presentation can affect the value by as much as one third.

The business needs to be presented in an organized, professional, and complete manner. The company, industry, and marketplace need to be explained thoroughly. The competitive strengths of the company need to be stressed.

In the same way in which cleaning up and repairing a piece of real estate increases its value, cleaning up and repairing a business increases its value. However, more than just the facilities must be included in the cleanup. The records and documentation of the company are as important, if not more important, than the facilities.

The presentation to the buyer should emphasize the things that interest the buyer. While it is difficult to know what any one buyer is most interested in, there are some things that interest nearly all buyers. Buyers are interested in the future—they want to know how the business will expand, they want to know what the company's future profits can be. They also want to know about proprietary and competitive advantages which they can use to help the business grow.

Chapters 6 and 7 discuss in detail what needs to be done to prepare a business for sale. Chapters 9, 10, and 11 discuss preparing the documentation necessary for a good presentation to a buyer.

EXPLAIN THE PAST, SELL THE FUTURE

A company is valuable because of what it can do in the future, not because of what it has done in the past. A buyer acquires a company based on expectations of the future. If buyers believed that the future of a company would be worse than the past, they would not be interested in buying it.

In the documentation and in discussions with potential buyers, one goal should be to intelligently show how the future of the company can be enhanced. The presentations and documentation should explain what has happened in the past and sell the company's future capabilities.

MARKET CONDITIONS AND VALUE

The company is part of a larger regional and national economic system. Activity in this economic environment can affect value. Regardless of the success or failure of the company, if the market is up, the value of the company will also be up. If the market is down, the value of the business will follow.

All other things being equal, the company is worth more in a period of low interest rates and conversely is worth less in a period of high interest rates. The company is worth less during an economic recession and conversely it is worth more during a period of economic growth. Be aware of general economic perceptions in the marketplace—they can have an effect on value.

WHEN TO USE AND HOW TO DEAL WITH PROFESSIONAL APPRAISERS

Under certain circumstances it may be a good idea to have a professional business appraiser value the business. A business appraiser can provide a fresh, unbiased look at the company. The appraiser's independent opinion gives the seller an idea of what to expect from buyers regarding price. Many business owners like to have an appraisal done prior to deciding whether to sell the business.

There are several guidelines to follow to assure that you obtain a quality appraisal that will assist in selling the business. Select someone with several years of valuation experience. Ask for references and check them out. Business valuation is complex and requires someone committed to the field. Don't make the mistake of hiring a part-time appraiser. It is also a good idea to seek an appraiser who is a member of the American Society of Appraisers (ASA). The ASA trains and certifies business appraisers. To become a member of the ASA the appraiser must have a minimum of two years full-time experience and must pass a comprehensive business valuation examination.

If possible, talk with more than one appraiser. Appraisers have different personalities and approach appraisal assignments differently. The experience, level of expertise, and cost of appraisers varies widely. Find one you feel comfortable with. Remember that the presentation to the appraiser, just like the presentation to the buyer, will affect the conclusion of value.

Make sure the appraiser is familiar with the company's industry and geographic area. Each industry is different. A business appraiser who is unfamiliar with the industry may fail to properly consider significant valuation issues.

Determine in advance the cost of the appraisal. The cost of an appraisal varies significantly among appraisers. Some charge a flat fee; others charge an hourly rate for their services.

Pick an appraiser who is familiar with the laws, regulations, and court rulings affecting business valuations. It is also to your advantage if the appraiser is experienced in defending his or her appraisals before the Internal Revenue Service and in court.

Finally, make sure that you have a formal agreement with the appraiser that defines what property is being appraised, the date of valuation, the purpose of the appraisal, the cost, the form of the appraisal report, and the expected time schedule.

Section 3
The Sales Literature

Chapter 9

The Sales Literature and the Company Summary

SALES LITERATURE

A buyer makes his or her decision about the desirability and value of a business based on the information available. The primary sources of information include conversations with the owner and the owner's agents, the on-site facility inspection, and the selling documents which the seller provides. The selling documents, or sales literature, includes all documents given to the seller. A company description, product brochure, financial statement, or price list are all considered to be selling documents.

Perhaps with the exception of a brief telephone conversation, the selling documents contain the first information about the company that the buyer will see. The completeness, accuracy, and relevance of the information contained in the selling documents will have a significant impact on the buyer's decision.

In days past, buyers were operations oriented—they made purchase decisions based on the equipment and facilities of the business. Today, buyers are oriented towards the financial and documentary aspects of the business—they make purchase decisions based on the documentation and records of the company.

The sales literature consists primarily of two documents: the company summary and the detailed business analysis. The company summary is a brief document of two to four pages. It is the initial sales tool which concisely describes the company. The document emphasizes those items that would spark a buyer's interest. A potential buyer will form an initial impression about the company from this summary. It is the lure that makes the buyer want to find out more about the company. The company summary should be written in a fashion that will allow prospective buyers to quickly obtain a grasp of the true nature of the business.

The second document is the detailed business analysis (DBA). If the company summary is the lure then the DBA is the hook. The DBA should answer all of the buyer's questions and convince the buyer to buy the business. This document provides the buyer with a detailed description of the operations of the company. The buyer learns about the history of the business as well as the history of the industry and marketplace. The DBA tells the buyer about the financial success of the company. From the DBA the buyer forms opinions and feelings about the strengths and weaknesses of the firm, about how successful the company has been, and about how successful it might be under new ownership. The purpose of the DBA is twofold; first, it informs the buyer about the business; second, it sells the business to the buyer.

A significant part of the DBA is a presentation of the true financial condition and profitability of the company. (Chapter 11, "Adjusting Financial Statements," presents a discussion of how the financial statements of the company should be presented to a buyer.) Often the financial statements of a privately held company do not show an accurate picture of the company's true financial success. Historically the owner has kept profits low to reduce taxes. The owner may take out salary and benefits which are greater than would be paid to an employee manager. The balance sheet of the company is based on the historic cost of the assets, not their current fair market value. Frequently the owner's personal investments and outside business interests are mixed in with the business. For these reasons it is necessary to adjust or restructure the financial statements prior to presenting them to a potential buyer. (A detailed description and outline of the DBA is presented in Chapter 10.)

Preparing the Selling Documents

The selling documents should be prepared in a positive and optimistic manner. This is the time to highlight the attributes of the business. The business must be presented well if it is to be sold at a premium price.

The documents must also be fair. Identify the weaknesses of the company as well as its strengths. Don't present false or misleading information. If information is misrepresented, the buyer will find out. Every important piece of information will be verified by the buyer before the sale is finalized.

The selling documents may be long and detailed. The task of compiling the information and writing the documents can be laborious. Sellers often question whether it is necessary to go to all the effort. It may be possible to sell the business without such reports, but a well prepared selling document gives the seller an edge in the marketplace. Well-prepared documents encourage buyers to give the company a second look when they might not otherwise.

When determining the level of effort used to prepare these documents, consider two things. The first is the type of documentation comparable companies use. Your documents should be as good or better than those used by others. The second item is the sophistication of the buyer. The level of quality demanded by the buyer is directly related to his or her level of sophistication. If you plan to sell to a large corporation or a group of experienced investors you need to have documentation that will meet their needs.

THE MARKETING PACKAGE

The initial package provided to a prospective buyer consists of four items. These include a letter of introduction, the company summary, a confidentiality agreement, and a buyer information sheet.

The letter explains that the package is in reference to a company that is for sale, introduces the contact person, and explains the other documents included in the package. The company summary presents to the prospective buyer information about the company. The confidentiality agreement is to be signed by the buyer. By signing, the buyer agrees that all the information provided about the company will be confidential and will not be shared with anyone. The buyer also agrees that the information will be used only for considering the acquisition of your company and for no other purpose.

The buyer information sheet requests some basic information about the buyer personally as well as his or her company. The process of buyer prequalification begins with the information from this sheet. It can be determined whether the buyer has the resources to purchase the company and whether or not the seller wants to deal with the buyer. Buyers sometimes hesitate to provide information. However, a buyer wants to know everything about the company and the seller. It is reasonable for the seller to demand relevant information about the buyer.

THE COMPANY SUMMARY

The company summary is the initial sales brochure used to market the company. It is a blind document of two to four pages, which accurately and briefly describes the company. (It is called a blind document because it does not specifically identify the company.) It is informative to the buyer. It emphasizes the strengths of the company. It tells a buyer why the company is a good investment. The company summary presents a summary of the financial condition and performance of the company. Finally it identifies who to contact to obtain more information.

A blind company summary allows you to safely market your company without the disruption caused when word gets out that the company is for sale. Relevant information is given so the buyer can determine his or her level of interest, but the company's confidentiality is maintained. Only after an interested buyer has met the seller's approval and agreed to maintain confidentiality will the name of the company be revealed.

A company summary should address these ten key areas:

1. Introduction
2. Key Points of Interest
3. History and Organization
4. Business Description
5. Product Description
6. Marketing Efforts
7. Financial Summary
8. Personnel/Employees
9. Facilities
10. Future Expectations

The introduction provides the general location of the company (state or region), the industry in which the company participates, the number of employees, and the name, phone number, and address of the contact person.

The key points of interest section summarizes in a brief, easy-to-read format those items which would be most significant to a buyer. This section is most commonly written in short sentences which are direct and to the point. All other sections consist of one or two descriptive paragraphs.

The history and organization section describes the age of the company, the type of organization, the number of owners, the number of locations, and other similar information.

The business description and product description sections describe briefly the nature of the company and the significant product lines.

The marketing efforts section describes the sales, marketing, and advertising efforts of the company.

The financial summary section includes a brief summary of the income statement and balance sheet of the company. The emphasis is on the sales and profitability of the company.

The personnel/employees section describes the workforce. Any unique characteristics or special training requirements should be mentioned. The business owner's involvement in the company may also be described.

The facilities section describes briefly the facilities and equipment of the company, including information on ownership, capacity, condition, and leases.

The future expectations section describes the growth and development expected by the owner in the future. In addition to a verbal description, pro forma revenue or profit projections are often included.

The outline above is only a starting point. You may decide to add or delete some categories to best present your own company. Do whatever needs to be done to best present the company—the better the presentation, the higher the level of success. Exhibits 9–1 and 9–2 provide examples of two company summaries.

Exhibit 9–1
Company Summary—Example One

Type of Business: Direct Mail Publishing Company

Location: California

Number of Employees: 5

Contact: Mr. Seller's Agent
1234 Park Lane
Los Angeles, CA
(123) 456-7890

Key Points of Interest

Sells exclusively to financial services professionals.

Markets through direct mail and periodical advertisements.

Mails over 750,000 direct mail pieces per year.

Pretax profits are in excess of 20% of sales.

Average annual revenue growth of over 15% for the past
four years.

History and Organization

Founded in 19XX, the company is solely owned by the
president. The owner is an author who saw a need for
a publisher to serve the financial services professional
exclusively. The company has been very successful at
selecting good titles and effectively marketing to reduce
expenses.

(Exhibit continues)

Exhibit 9–1 (Continued)

Product Description

The company currently has a large selection of books in
   print, with exclusive rights to all. The company owns
   no copyrights. All books are selected with the needs of
   the financial services professional in mind. The
   company plans to add five to eight titles per year over
   the next three years.

Marketing Efforts

The company mails over 750,000 pieces of direct mail
   annually. It also regularly places advertisements in
   periodicals and trade journals.

Financial Summary (000's)

	Fiscal Year End: Dec. 31			
Income statement*	19XX	19XX	19XX	19XX
Sales	1,550	1,812	2,091	2,430
Gross Profit	634	691	838	929
	41%	38%	40%	38%
Pretax Profits	273	386	462	510
	18%	21%	22%	21%

Exhibit 9–1 (Continued)

Balance Sheet [*]   *Dec. 31, 19XX*

Current Assets	788
Fixed Assets	<u>110</u>
Total Assets	898
Current Liabilities	117
Long-Term Liabilities	0
Owner's Equity	<u>781</u>
Total Liabilities & Equity	898

[*] The financial statements have been adjusted to reflect the true earning power of the firm. Adjustments have been made for excess owner's earnings and for other relevant items. Privately held companies seek to reduce profits in order to reduce income taxes. Details of the adjustments are available from the contact person.

Personnel/Employees

The company employs five people including the owner. All employees, except the owner, are expected to remain with the company. The owner desires to remain for an extended transition period of twelve to eighteen months.

Facilities

The company occupies 4500 square feet of office space leased at $4,900 per month. The current three-year lease has eighteen months remaining.

Future Expectations

Management believes that the firm has just begun to penetrate this market and that substantial growth opportunities exist. With the addition of five to eight titles per year, the company's revenue should double in three years to nearly $5,000,000, with pretax profits in excess of $1,000,000.

Exhibit 9–2
Company Summary—Example Two

Type of Business: Wire Harness Assembler

Location: Illinois

Number of Employees: 105

Contact: Mr. Contact Person
1234 Park Lane
Chicago. IL
(123) 456-7890

Key Points of Interest

Sells to the electronic equipment and the automotive industries.

Over 25 years in business.

Pretax profits in excess of 12% of revenue.

Provides complete wire harness design services.

Excellent long-term relationships with major customers.

History and Organization

Founded in the early Sixties, the company has two equal owners. One is the original founder, who is approaching retirement. The other is the son of a previous owner. The company has been very successful at designing quality wire harnesses and cables that can be produced quickly at minimal cost.

Business Description

The company designs and assembles wire harnesses and cables. The company specializes in small and medium-sized production runs. All jobs are done on a bid basis.

Exhibit 9–2 (Continued)

Business Description (Continued)

The company has maintained excellent long-term relationships (over ten years) with its five major customers. These customers account for approximately 60% of the total revenue of the company.

Product Description

The wire harnesses and cables which the company designs and assembles are used in automobiles and in electronic equipment such as typewriters and computer printers. The company has an automated design process which allows it to efficiently design and produce these items.

Marketing Efforts

The company has two estimators which prepare bids for all jobs. The senior owner is also involved in the sales and marketing efforts with the company's five major customers. All sales are made to customers within 250 miles of the company.

Financial Summary (000's)

		Fiscal Year End: Dec. 31		
Income statement*	19XX	19XX	19XX	19XX
Sales	3,909	4,066	4,887	4,745
Gross Profit	1,133	1,138	1,418	1,329
	29%	28%	29%	28%
Pretax Profits	446	481	623	584
	11%	12%	13%	12%

(Exhibit continues)

Exhibit 9–2 (Continued)

Balance Sheet *   *Dec. 31, 19XX*

Current Assets	1,239
Fixed Assets	726
Total Assets	1,965
Current Liabilities	1,063
Long-Term Liabilities	239
Owner's Equity	663
Total Liabilities & Equity	1,965

* The financial statements have been adjusted to reflect the true earning power of the firm. Adjustments have been made for excess owner's earnings and for other relevant items. Privately held companies seek to reduce profits in order to reduce income taxes. Details of the adjustments are available from the contact person.

Personnel/Employees

The company currently has 105 employees including the owners. The key managers of the company include the general manager, office manager, two estimators, and four foremen. The senior owner, who desires to retire, functions as the general manager. The other owner is a foremen.

Facilities

The company occupies 12,800 square feet in a production facility leased from the owners of the company. The current lease rate is $5,500 per month. The lease is month-to-month. The facility is being operated at approximately 65% of capacity on a two-shift basis.

Future Expectations

Management expects the continued success of the company. Historic growth has been achieved with only minimal marketing effort. Opportunities exist for rapid growth with aggressive owners and increased marketing efforts.

Chapter 10
The Detailed Business Analysis

The detailed business analysis (DBA) is an in-depth report which a buyer uses to thoroughly analyze the company. Based on the information in the DBA, a buyer can decide whether or not to pursue the acquisition of the company. The DBA should be written to anticipate and answer as many of the buyers questions as possible.

The detailed business analysis is similar to an offering memorandum or detailed business plan. However, it is important that the DBA is not called an offering memorandum. The business is not being sold to the public, and the seller is not registering the securities with the Securities and Exchange Commission. The seller is not subject to the rules and regulations of registered securities and therefore, to avoid confusion, should not use the terminology associated with registered securities.

The DBA is a complete and thorough presentation about the company. It may vary in length from twenty to more than one hundred pages. The DBA describes in detail the history, operations, and projected future of the company. After reading the DBA the buyer should have a good understanding of all aspects of the company, including its competitive position in the marketplace.

The company summary is provided to all potential buyers. Those who ask for additional information after seeing the company summary are sent a copy of the DBA. Prior to sending the DBA to an interested buyer the seller must:

1. Guarantee the confidentiality of the document;
2. Prequalify the buyer to ascertain whether he or she is able to purchase the business;
3. Be confident that the seller and the buyer are able to do business together; and
4. Establish what is and is not acceptable regarding contact with company personnel.

CONFIDENTIALITY

Maintaining the confidentiality of the DBA is important. The DBA contains sensitive financial and other proprietary information about the company. This information, if put in the wrong hands, could compromise the competitive position of the company. In an effort to assure confidentiality the seller must demand that all potential buyers sign and agree to abide by a confidentiality agreement. (In Chapter 14, "Dealing with the Buyer," a detailed discussion of confidentiality agreements is presented.)

QUALIFYING THE BUYER

Qualifying a potential buyer is a difficult but necessary task. Detailed information about the company should not be given out to just anyone, and time is too valuable to waste on any buyer who does not have the means to buy the company. It is reasonable and proper to ask the buyer for a resume and financial information. It is important to know if the buyer has the financial ability to buy the company and the technical or management expertise to run it.

If the buyer is hesitant to provide this information, the buyer should be reminded that he or she is asking for confidential information about the company. If the buyer and seller are going to develop the mutual respect necessary for a professional relationship, they need to know about each other. The seller shouldn't merely give out information—the seller should *trade* information. A buyer who will not provide adequate information is either not serious about buying or is unable to buy. (A detailed discussion about how to qualify a buyer is presented in Chapter 14, "Dealing with the Buyer.")

BUYER-SELLER RELATIONSHIP

The personal chemistry between the seller and the buyer is a major factor in a successful sale. If there is not quality relationship with mutual respect, the sale may fall apart. Every seller can identify potential buyers that they have no desire to deal with. Buyers and sellers usually have strong personalities; throughout their business careers they have identified types of people that they will not do business with. If the buyer's personality is in conflict with the seller's, recognize it and deal with it up front. If the relationship cannot be improved, the deal will not work. The chemistry or compatibility between the buyer and seller is just as important as the price and terms of the transaction.

BUYER CONTACT WITH COMPANY PERSONNEL

The DBA often identifies the key management of the company. A buyer may want to contact these managers directly with questions about certain aspects of the company's operations. An understanding with the buyer regarding proper contact procedures should be established. This is especially critical in a situation of confidentiality where some or all of the key managers may not know that the company is for sale.

AUTHORSHIP OF THE DETAILED BUSINESS ANALYSIS

Who writes the detailed business analysis? It can be written by the business broker, the owner of the company, one or more employees of the company, an outside consultant, or a combination of all of the above. The report is a long and detailed one. The information in the report will come from many different sources. Perhaps the sales people will provide information about sales and marketing, the accountants will provide the financial analysis, the engineers or research and development people will provide the information about technology, and the operations people will provide information about manufacturing process and capacity.

Usually the more sources involved in providing information, the better the report. Information coming from many sources will enhance the completeness and detail of the report. Regardless of who provides the information or who authors the report the business owner should have the final review and approval of its content—after all, he or she will be the one who will benefit from the sale. Furthermore, the owner is the one who must warrant to the buyer that the information in the DBA is accurate and complete.

If the company is being sold by an intermediary, the broker or the broker's staff will probably write the DBA. However, it should be written with information provided by the seller. Often a seller will use employees of the company to write or provide information for sections of the DBA; however, the seller will usually not tell them the information will be used to sell the business. The seller tells them the information is needed for a marketing plan, business plan, or a report for a banker or a management consultant.

The detailed business analysis is the most important selling tool used. Regardless of who writes the report, the seller must be involved. His or her review will help assure that the information is complete, accurate, and presents the company in a positive way.

WRITING THE DETAILED BUSINESS ANALYSIS

A sample outline for the detailed business analysis follows. An attempt has been made to make this outline as complete as possible. As the DBA is being created for an individual company, sections will be added, deleted, or modified to fit the unique characteristics of the company, industry, and marketplace.

A. Company Description
     General Business Description
     Strengths and Weaknesses
     History
     Ownership
     Organization
     Products/Services
     Markets and Customers
     Sales and Marketing
     Pricing
     Competition
     Backlog
     Facilities
     Capacity
     Suppliers and Contracts
     Hours of Operation
     Employees
     Seasonality
     Government Regulation

B. Industry Analysis
     Industry Structure
     Industry Growth
     Competitive Factors
     Industry Trends

C. Market Analysis
     Market Structure
     Market Growth
     Market Trends

D. Financial Review
     Financial Statement Analysis
     Pretax Cash Flow
     Financial Statement Review
     Financial Ratio Analysis
     Summary and Conclusion

E. Future Expectations
   Marketing Plans
   New Products
   Research and Development
   Projected Growth
   Pro Forma Financial Statements
   Summary and Conclusions

F. Appendices
   Company Financial Statements
   Product Literature
   Resumes of Key Management
   Asset Lists/Appraisals

The level of detail and effort necessary for an adequate report varies from company to company. A larger, more detailed report is necessary for a larger, more complex company. A small business would typically sell to a less sophisticated buyer who does not need as detailed a report.

Find out what documentation is being used to sell similar businesses. Be certain the DBA you create is the best available.

THE DETAILED BUSINESS ANALYSIS

A discussion of each section in the detailed business analysis follows.

Company Description

The company description section of the DBA is the first major section. Its purpose is to provide the reader with basic information about the company. It includes information such as: what the company does, what the different product lines are, where the company is located, where the branch offices are, who the competitors are, how the company compares to the competition, who owns the company, how many employees the company has, when the company was formed, how its products are sold, what type of advertising the company uses, how its staff is organized, how many customers it has, who its primary customers are, what government agencies regulate the company, and what technology the company uses.

When outlining and writing this section, imagine that you are the buyer. Include the information that would answer the questions you would have. The section should be formatted into subsections for each of the categories. The paragraphs should be short and to the point. The goal is to provide a wealth of detailed information in a concise manner.

General Business Description: This is a brief section of two or three paragraphs. It provides the name and address of the company. Also included is a description of the business, what it is, and what it does.

Strengths and Weaknesses: In this section the major strengths and weaknesses of the company are listed in a brief "bullet" format. This is similar to the strengths and weaknesses section of the company presented in the company summary. The presentation may be identical to the company summary or it may be expanded. Some examples of company strengths might be:

- Above-average revenue growth
- Above-average profitability
- A reputation for high quality
- Owning a patented or proprietary technology or process
- Having a new modernized facility
- Having an established experienced sales network

Some examples of company weaknesses might be:

- Undercapitalization
- Old/obsolete facility and equipment
- A recent new product failure
- The lack of an aggressive, active sales and marketing program

History: A buyer is interested in knowing when, how, and by whom the business was formed. Also included in this section is a chronology of significant business events. These events include such things as facility changes, branch facility additions, significant changes in ownership (especially when the current owner acquired control), changes in management, dates of new product line introductions, and the development of patents or technology advances.

Don't intentionally leave out items that are not desirable. The closing of an unprofitable facility, the elimination of a product line, or a fire at the plant are all part of the history and show that the company has the ability to adapt to the competitive environment and handle unforeseen serious problems.

A detailed history is not necessary—describe only major items that show a history of the company's growth and development.

Ownership: In this section include a list of all the shareholders of the company, along with the number of shares and percentage ownership which they have. If there are so many shareholders that a complete list is cumbersome or impractical, include the total number of shareholders and a list of the significant shareholders. A significant shareholder is someone who owns more than 5 percent of the outstanding stock of the company.

Organization: Describe the legal and operational organization of the company. Legally the company is either a sole proprietorship, partnership, or corporation. If the company is a corporation, provide the date of incorporation.

Operationally the company can be organized in many different ways. Provide an organization chart showing all of the key departments and managers. Describe the reporting relationships so the buyer can see who makes the important decisions.

It is also important to show expertise and depth of management. Include a paragraph describing each of the key managers of the company. List their age, health, education, experience, and expertise. Describe any management replacement or backup plans which may exist. Let the buyer know that the company has good management talent and has made provisions to assure that trained and talented managers will be available in the future.

Products/Services: In this section the major product lines of the company should be identified and described. Identify the contribution of each product line to revenue and profit. Discuss the customer service, warranty, and credit terms offered with each product line. Discuss how each product line is unique and what its competitive advantages are. Identify any new products which are being developed or are planned for release in the near future.

Markets and Customers: Describe an "average" customer, if possible. If the customers fall into several categories, describe each category. Tell how many active customers the company has. The definition of an active customer varies from industry to industry but it is usually defined as any customer that purchases at least once a year.

Describe why customers buy your product and explain the end use of the product. Does the company sell to the end user or to a middleman?

Explain whether the company's products are purchased on a one-time basis or repeatedly by the customers. A buyer will want to know what percentage of your customers are repeat customers and what portion of revenue they account for.

If there are any customers that consistently account for more than 10 percent of the company's annual revenue, they need to be identified. Explain who they are, how long they have been buying, any sales agreements that exist, and what the company is doing to ensure it keeps the customer.

Sales and Marketing: This section answers many questions. How are the products of the company advertised and sold? How many salespeople are there? Where are they located? How do they sell? Are they paid salary or commission? Are yellow page ads used? Are magazine or trade journals advertisements used? What about newspaper, radio, or television ads? Does the company use telemarketing, direct mail, or catalog advertising? How important are referrals? Does the company participate in trade shows? Describe which of these advertising methods are used, the extent of their use, and their effectiveness. Explain how much the company spends each year on advertising and why.

Pricing: The buyer needs to know how the company's prices are set. Explain the company's pricing philosophy. Is the company a price leader or is it a price discounter? Are products priced on a cost-plus formula? Are they priced based on a desired profit margin? Are prices set based on what the market will bear? Are prices determined by bid or negotiation with the customer? Is the industry such that a leader sets the prices and others follow?

Understanding the pricing methodology helps the buyer assess the competitiveness of the industry and where the company is positioned. This is critical information which the buyer needs to help plan for the future of the company under new ownership.

Competition: No intelligent buyer will acquire a company without first having a knowledge of the businesses with which that company competes. Providing this information in the DBA accomplishes two things. The buyer's job is made easier—the seller is doing part of the buyer's research. Also, the seller is informing the buyer that he or she knows the competitors and their situation. The company being sold has addressed the competitive situation of the industry and market and has full knowledge of where it fits.

The information provided about the company's competitors does not need to be detailed, but should be accurate and pertinent. If there are many competitors it is not necessary to provide complete information on all of them. It is recommended that the seller identify two or three market leaders and the three or four competitors most comparable to the company and provide information on these companies.

The information on competitors should include, if possible, the name of the company, the address, the type of business, revenue figures including trends, number of employees, sales territory, sales methods and strategies, future growth expectations, and company attributes which the competitor considers its strengths.

Backlog: If the company has a normal backlog of orders, explain how the backlog system works and what the normal amount of backlog is. If the backlog is seasonal, explain the seasonality. Specify the current level of backlog and explain why it is greater or smaller than the normal level.

Facilities: List all the facilities of the company including corporate offices, manufacturing facilities, sales offices, and branch offices. Provide the address, date of original occupancy, purpose of the facility, size of the facility, lease rate, lease expiration date, whether the lease can be assigned and other relevant information.

Capacity: The information in this section lets the buyer know how much the business can grow before expansion is required and, if known, what the cost of expansion would be. Let the buyer know what level of revenue the facility could support if it were at full capacity, and what level of operations the machinery and equipment could support at full capacity.

Inform the buyer of the current capacity utilization of the facility, the machinery, and the equipment. If the business is currently being operated on a one-shift basis, discuss whether it could be expanded to two or three shifts.

If any plans for expansion have been considered it may be appropriate to describe them. Indicate what the expansion would include in facility additions, equipment additions, and cost. Be sure to identify the amount of increased capacity which the expansion will provide.

Suppliers and Contracts: Identify the company's major suppliers of raw materials, and list any alternative sources of supply. Also inform the buyer of any contractual arrangements with suppliers.

The buyer needs to know not only about contracts with suppliers, but contracts with customers. If any sales contracts with customers exist, provide details of these contracts as well.

Hours of Operation: This is a critical item for retail oriented businesses. List the company's hours of business. Specify the hours for each day of the week if there is any variation.

Employees: In this section tell the buyer how many employees there are in the entire company and in each department or location. Provide an explanation of any special skills or training necessary for any particular position. Discuss whether there is an adequate supply of trained employees in the available workforce. If there is not, explain what the company does to acquire and train employees.

This section should also address unions. If the workers are not organized, state it. If the workers are organized, provide information detailing what employees are unionized, what unions and locals are involved, when the last contract was negotiated, and when it expires. Also provide a summary of past relations with the unions. If there have been any strikes, lockouts, or other work interruptions in the past several years, provide details about them.

Seasonality: If the operations of the business are seasonal, explain it in this section. Provide information as to the reason for the seasonality. Explain the degree of seasonality and identify busy and slow periods. Explain what the company has done to deal with seasonality. Describe the actions the company has taken to smooth out operations.

Government Regulation: Let the buyer know what government agencies regulate the company and the relationship which exists with those agencies. Identify the licenses and approvals which the company has obtained. This information is important: it tells the buyer that the government has given the company a clean bill of health. Few things muddy the water like regulatory problems—assure the buyer that the company is without conflicts in this regard.

Industry Analysis

The purpose of this section of the DBA is to provide the buyer with an understanding of the industry in which the company participates. From this section the buyer can determine where the company fits in the industry and if the competitive makeup of the industry is a desirable one.

Industry Structure: The structure of an industry is defined as the relationship and makeup of the industry participants. How many companies are part of the industry, and how do they relate to each other? Is it an industry with a few leaders and a lot of followers? Is it an industry with only a few leaders and no followers? Is the industry comprised of many small and medium-sized firms, lacking large industry leaders?

Industry Growth: This section contains relatively straightforward statistics about the historic growth of the industry and its projected future growth. Explain why growth has been what it has been. If there are major industry segments, then present statistics by segment, if possible. A comparison of the company to the industry should also be provided. If the company has grown faster or slower than the industry, offer reasons why. At what rate has the industry grown in the past? What is the expected growth of the industry in the future? What stage of development is the industry in? Is it a growth industry or a mature industry?

Competitive Factors: Competitive factors within the industry are very important. Do companies compete based on price, service, quality, technology, or some other basis? Which competitive factor is most important? Which factors are not important? How does the company measure up in each area?

Industry Trends: This section describes the industry's past development and the changes expected in the future. The buyer wants to know strategically what is happening in the industry. Is the technology in the industry changing? Is the number of companies in the industry growing or declining? What is happening in the area of government regulation and legislation?

Market Analysis

The market analysis gives the buyer the same information about the market that the industry section provides about the industry. The market is defined as the customers who purchase the product and the end users of the product.

Market Structure: This section defines how the market is organized. Are there many market participants or a few? Who are the dominant customers in the market? How does the market use the product? What characteristics of the product are most important to the market? How does the market purchase the product?

Market Growth: This section contains relatively straightforward statistics about the historic growth of the market and the projected future growth. Also explain why growth has been what it has been and what assumptions were used in projecting future growth.

Market Trends: This section presents the market's past development and the changes expected in the future.

Financial Review

The financial review is a critical section of the report for two reasons. First, the primary function of a business is to provide a profit or return on investment. It is from the financial review section that the buyer will form opinions about the company's potential profits. Second, most buyers are oriented more towards the financial end of a business. For these reasons, this section must be well researched and professionally presented.

The financial review section is divided into five subsections. In the first subsection, *Financial Statement Adjustments*, the adjustments necessary to show the true profitability of the company are explained and presented. (Adjusting financial statements is a detailed and complicated task, examined at greater length in Chapter 11, "Adjusting Financial Statements.")

In the second subsection, *Pretax Cash Flow*, the historic cash flow of the company is computed and presented.

The third subsection, *Financial Statement Review*, presents the historic financial trends of the company. Any significant variations in the historical financial operations are explained.

The fourth subsection, *Financial Ratio Analysis*, presents the financial ratios for the company and the industry. Trends in the ratios are examined and explained and a comparison between the company and the industry is presented.

In the fifth and final subsection, *Summary and Conclusion*, the profitability, cash flow, and financial strengths of the company are summarized. The key issues of the other subsections are reiterated and a conclusion regarding the financial strength of the company is presented.

Financial Statement Adjustments: This section is usually divided into three parts. The first is an introduction. In the introduction the reasons why financial statement adjustments are needed are explained. In the second part the adjustments to the income statements are presented and explained. In the third part the adjustments to the balance sheet are presented and explained.

Even though the financial statement adjustments are presented in the financial schedules, it is important to present each of the adjustments in the text. The adjustment should be explained, the sources of the figures should be cited, and the calculations should be presented. The presentation is more effective when the buyer reads the explanation in the text and then sees the adjustments in the schedules.

The financial schedules which present the adjusted income statement and adjusted balance sheet are included as part of this section.

Pretax Cash Flow Analysis: A buyer buys a business because of the cash flow that can be earned from the business. Therefore, a cash flow analysis is important. The presentation should include a discussion of the computation as well as a schedule showing the calculations. The pretax cash flow is defined as follows:

	19XX	19XX	19XX
Adjusted Operating Profit	XXX	XXX	XXX
Plus: Non-cash Expenses			
Depreciation	XX	XX	XX
Amortization	X	X	X
Other Non-cash Expenses	XX	XX	XX
Subtotal	XXX	XXX	XXX
Pretax Cash Flow	XXXX	XXXX	XXXX

The pretax cash flow should be calculated for each period presented in the income statement analysis.

Financial Statement Review: In this section the buyer is presented with a discussion of the historic financial performance of the company. The review is usually in two major sections, an income statement review and a balance sheet review.

The income statement section presents a discussion of the major income statement categories such as revenue, cost of sales, gross profit, operating expenses, and operating profit. A discussion of the growth rate, trends, and significant items affecting each category would be presented, along with an explanation of significant variances from year to year.

The balance sheet review section would discuss the major balance sheet categories such as cash, accounts receivable, inventory, fixed asset, other assets, accounts payable, accrued liabilities, long-term liabilities, and owner's equity. A discussion of the significant increases or decreases of each account would be included. An explanation of the company's policies pertaining to inventory, accounts receivable, and accounts payable management should also be included in this section.

Often in this section only the most recent balance sheet is presented. If this is the case, then a schedule with additional balance sheet information for prior years should be included. This schedule should present the important balance sheet accounts for each of the last three to five years. This schedule does not have to present a complete balance sheet; it needs only to present the key account balances which are discussed in the text.

When the fixed asset account is discussed, the capital expenditures of the company for the past three to five years should be presented and explained. The historic level of capital expenditures is important to the buyer, as it provides some information about the effective age of the fixed assets and the expected level of capital expenditures in the future. A buyer should understand the reasons behind increases or decreases in revenue and expenses over the past few years, as well as how the company manages its balance sheet's asset and liability accounts.

Financial Ratio Analysis: Financial ratios are used to judge the financial health and to analyze the operating efficiency of the firm. Financial ratios are most useful when compared against an industry standard.

A ratio presentation of three years is adequate. This allows the buyer to see both the company's past trends and its current status.

There are literally dozens of ratios which can be used; however, there are about ten ratios which are commonly understood and which should be presented as a minimum. Additional ratios which are particularly useful to the industry or a buyer may also be presented.

It is best if the basic ratios are broken down into three categories: profitability, liquidity, and operational efficiency. The profitability ratios include return on sales, return on assets, and return on equity. The liquidity ratios include the current ratio, the quick ratio, and the long-term debt to equity ratio. Operational efficiency ratios include inventory turnover, accounts receivable collection period, payables turnover, and sales to total asset turnover.

The ratios should be presented in a schedule which allows the buyer to see the historic trends of the company, as well the company's ratios compared to those of the industry. Describe the historic trends of the company, and explain any significant variations between company and industry ratios.

Industry ratios are usually obtained from one of three sources: industry associations; Robert Morris and Associates; and Dun & Bradstreet. Many industry associations compile industry financial ratios. If these are available they should be used. They are usually considered to be the most reliable. Robert Morris and Associates publishes an annual publication titled "RMA Annual Statement Studies," intended primarily for use by the banking industry. It provides financial ratios for many industries, categorized by the Federal Government's Standard Industry Classification (SIC) code. "RMA Annual Statement Studies" is often available at the public library.

The Dun & Bradstreet publication, "Key Business Ratios," also provides financial ratios for different industries based on SIC codes. It is more complete than the Robert Morris publication. However, it is usually not available at the public library and is quite expensive to purchase.

Summary and Conclusion: In this section the profitability, cash flow, historic growth, balance sheet trends, and financial ratio performance of the company are all summarized and tied together. This subsection provides a good opportunity to creatively explain the financial strengths of the company. Conclusions regarding the financial strengths and weaknesses of the company should be presented and discussed.

Future Expectations

In this section, the company's possible plans for the future are revealed. Possible ways to enhance the future of the company and increase sales or profits are presented.

This section of the DBA is very fluid. The section must be adapted to the unique situation of the company being sold. The area of future opportunities is where the weaknesses of the company can be used to the company's advantage. If a buyer were to correct a weakness, such as inferior marketing efforts, then the future of the company could be enhanced significantly.

Six subsections are often included in this section. Each section is described below:

Marketing Plans: In this subsection future plans for the company's sales and marketing efforts are explained. Items such as an expanded salesforce, expanded market territory, and additional advertising efforts are presented. If the company has historically been oriented towards production or technology, then the expansion of marketing efforts could be an excellent area of opportunity for the buyer.

New Products: In this subsection any existing plans or ideas regarding new products, services or product enhancements are presented. The related costs, time of development, and projected revenue should also be presented.

Ideas for new products should be limited to products which are similar to and compatible with the existing product line. Products which are very costly to develop, introduce or which require a long period of time for development can be discussed but should not be included when revenue projections are developed.

Research and Development: Most companies invest in research and development in an effort to keep up with technology and develop future opportunities for the company. A discussion of the research and development efforts of the firm and the expected future benefits is important. If new products or technologies are being developed, or if a future patent or proprietary position is possible, let the buyer know that he or she is buying this opportunity. If R&D is being done which will result in lower manufacturing costs, discuss this and include the lower costs in the pro forma income statements.

Projected Growth: Develop a projection of revenue levels for three to five years into the future. In this projection be sure to consider the following: the historic growth of the company; the historic growth of the industry; the projected future growth of the industry; reasonable increases in marketing and advertising efforts; expansions into new market territories; the introduction of new products; and any other relevant items.

When developing this revenue projection, remember that a buyer will be skeptical of future growth which is greater than historic growth. Therefore, be sure that the assumptions which support the growth figures are reasonable and well documented. Faster growth in the future is reasonable if the industry is expected to grow faster or if expansion will increase sales. The key is to have good assumptions and present those assumptions well.

Another factor which will cause debate is the inclusion of new products, sales efforts, or other factors in the revenue projection. Buyers will argue that these are new efforts which will be undertaken and paid for by the buyer, not the seller. Why should the buyer pay the seller for efforts and expenditures which the buyer will make? The seller on the other hand argues that these are relatively minor, inexpensive new efforts. They are not the result of significant labor and expense by the buyer—they are simply the result of fine-tuning the already existing operations of the company. Both arguments are valid. The business owner must use sound judgment when deciding what to include when developing the revenue projections. The goal is an aggressive yet reasonable projection.

Pro Forma Financial Statements: Pro forma income statements are based on revenue projections. The purpose of the pro forma statements is to present the buyer with a level of potential profitability which can be earned in the future. The revenue, cost, and expense data which is necessary as part of the pro forma statements should be consistent with historic amounts.

Also included in the text of this section is a discussion of the assumptions used in developing the pro forma statements. Well-developed assumptions which are reasonable and on sound footing are very important when convincing a buyer to accept the pro forma statements.

The pro forma income statements are usually presented in a financial statement format. The assumptions are also presented as footnotes to this schedule.

Summary and Conclusions: A summary of the potential future of the company is presented. All of the previous sections are tied together. A buyer will always consider the future before acquiring a business; your depiction of the company's future provides the buyer with part of his or her own analysis. What the seller desires is to have the idea of realistic future growth presented to the buyer. By so doing, the buyer is guided to consider the business in a more favorable light. It also helps the seller convey the idea that the value of the business is based on the future of the business, and not on the past.

Remember when writing this section the subtle difference between reality and fantasy: the presentation of future expectations cannot include major changes in operation or unrealistic expansion. A seller should not ask a buyer to pay for that which does not exist. The purpose of this section of the DBA is to show the buyer what the business can be with just a little planning and effort.

SOURCES OF INFORMATION

Most of the information included in the DBA will come from the business itself. If the company maintains good records and has developed short-term and long-term budgets, marketing plans, and strategic plans, much of the necessary information will already be compiled. It needs only to be identified and perhaps updated and organized.

The sections of the DBA requiring outside sources are those which deal with information about the industry, the market, and the competitors. One must rely on outside sources for the information which is included in the sections on competitor analysis, industry analysis, and market analysis.

Competitor Analysis

The best sources of information about the company's competitors are the competitors themselves. Obtain copies of their sales brochures, catalogs, and company fact sheets. If the competitor is a public company, get copies of its quarterly, annual, and 10k reports. If you know the owner or a key employee of the company, call them and talk about the industry and their company. You may be able to glean insight about the competition from these casual conversations.

If you do not know anyone personally to contact, then call the sales manager, a salesman, or a public relations representative—it is their job to talk about the company. They are usually happy to talk about the company's sales efforts, strengths, and successes. This approach will yield detailed information about the competitor about 50 percent of the time.

Industry and Market Analysis

There are many sources for market and industry information. For some industries there is an abundance of information; for others there is very little published information. Often the task of obtaining good information about the market and the industry turns into a real research project. If industry statistics are not readily available, then one must gather information through research and interviews of industry experts.

Usually the best source of information is an industry trade association. The purpose of these organizations is to promote and assist in the development of the industry. They frequently can tell you about historical growth, projected future growth, technology changes, industry trends, regulatory requirements, industry segments, and other industry information. Trade associations are not only concerned with the condition of the industry, but also with the markets the industry serves. They frequently provide the same information about the market that they do about the industry.

Occasionally the association will not have all of the necessary information. In such instances they can often direct you to other sources. Association personnel usually know the industry and market experts. They can tell you who the leading industry consultants are, who compiles industry statistics, what other industry associations exist, and what industry trade journals are published.

If the company is a member of a trade association this is the place to start. However, there is often more than one trade association serving an industry. To locate the appropriate trade association consult the *Encyclopedia of Associations*, an annual publication which lists thousands of associations. It is indexed by name and subject. It is published by Gale Research, Inc., of Detroit, Michigan. This publication is available in many public libraries.

Another source to consult is industry trade journals. Nearly all industries have one or more magazines published specifically for the participants of that industry. Find out which journals relate to the industry in question, and obtain and review back issues. Many journals periodically print articles which present industry statistics. Often they interview industry experts about the state of the industry, trends, and the projected future growth of the industry.

The names of the editors, authors, and industry experts are often more important than the articles themselves. The journal editors are themselves industry experts. They can intelligently discuss trends and developments. They can also provide the names of additional sources or industry experts. It may also be beneficial to contact and interview the authors of relevant articles or experts quoted in or interviewed by the journals.

Among many other potential sources of market and industry data are the federal government and the public library.

The Department of Commerce and the Census Bureau compile an incredible array of statistics, many of which can be helpful. One useful publication is the "Industry Outlook," published annually by the Department of Commerce, which features reports on many different industries including historical sales and growth statistics as well as future projections. Furthermore, every industry report in "Industry Outlook" includes the name and telephone number of the author. You can call the government's experts on the industry and discuss the industry directly with them. A copy of "Industry Outlook" can be purchased directly from the Department of Commerce, and it frequently can be found in the public library.

Another way to get access to the government's treasury of information is to call the local number for United States Government information. Explain to the operator the information you want. You will be referred to the appropriate office. Surprisingly, this is a very effective method, although you should be prepared to make several calls. It usually takes three or four referrals before you are connected with the person who actually has the information.

A third way to get access to the government's store of information is to identify the nearest library that is a government depository. This means that the library keeps a large collection of government published information. These libraries are usually the largest public libraries or university libraries. Visit during off-peak hours so the librarian has time to help you. Most librarians enjoy helping people with specific research questions, and will guide you to everything available on the industry and market.

The public library is also a good source for market and industry data. Find a library with a large selection of business periodicals. Ask at the reference desk to be shown how to use the "Business Periodicals Index" or some other index which identifies all of the magazine and newspaper articles written about the market or industry in question. A review of these articles will usually provide the information needed.

Chapter 11
Adjusting Financial Statements

Privately held companies usually attempt to minimize reported profits in an effort to minimize taxes. The owner often receives a salary, benefits, and perquisites which are greater than what an employee manager would receive. Frequently income and expenses related to the owner's personal investments or outside business interests are included in the financial statements of the company. It is necessary to adjust the income statements in order to show the true profitability and financial condition of the business.

The balance sheet of the company also needs to be adjusted. Nonoperating assets frequently exist and need to be identified. Balance sheets are prepared based on the actual cost of assets. When selling a business the concern is not with the original cost of the assets but with their current fair market value. The adjusted balance sheet presents the current value of the owner's equity. When the adjusted financial statements are complete, an accurate presentation of the company's true financial performance is available for presentation to a buyer.

When adjusting the financial statements and calculating the amount of the various adjustments, be sure to keep accurate records. Buyers will want to verify that all adjustments are reasonable and accurate.

INCOME STATEMENT ADJUSTMENTS

In presenting financials to a buyer, long-term trends and stable financial performance are important. Usually a history of three to five years is adequate for this purpose.

The best way to present the adjusted financial statements is to start with the actual financial statements as they were originally prepared by the accountant. Each adjustment is then presented, along with a footnote which explains the adjustment. The resulting schedule presents the adjusted operating profit of the company. An example of an adjusted income statement is shown in Exhibit 11–1.

Adjustments made when restructuring the income statements can be classified in four areas: (1) owner related expenses, (2) nonrecurring expenses, (3) nonoperating income and expenses, and (4) organizational changes.

Owner Related Adjustments

One of the privileges of ownership is having control over the salary and benefits paid to the owner and the owner's family. Frequently salaries in excess of fair market salaries are paid and expensive perquisites are provided. The purpose of the adjustments in this area is to eliminate the excessive expenses and to present a more accurate profit figure.

The owner's salary must be reduced (or sometimes increased) to the fair market salary. The salary paid to other family members may also need adjustment. The level of expenditures on perks and benefits may need adjustment as well. The expenses for automobiles, travel, insurance, and other perks must be examined. Don't eliminate all expenses related to perks and benefits—leave in an adequate expense to cover the reasonable perks and benefits for the job.

Exhibit 11-1
Sample Company
Adjusted Income Statement
for the Years Ended December 31
($000)

	19XX		19XX		19XX	
Total Revenue	1,929	100.0%	2,226	100.0%	2,562	100.0%
Cost of Sales	842	43.6%	977	43.9%	1,086	42.4%
Gross Profit	1,087	56.4%	1,249	56.1%	1,476	57.6%
Operating Expenses	992	51.4%	1,135	51.0%	1,332	52.0%
Operating Income	95	4.9%	114	5.1%	144	5.6%
Other Income/(Expense)	22	1.1%	(12)	–0.5%	27	1.1%
Pretax Income (per books)	117	6.1%	102	4.6%	171	6.7%
Adjustments						
Owner Related Items (1)	198	10.3%	237	10.6%	229	8.9%
Nonrecurring Items (2)	17	0.9%	0	0.0%	21	0.8%
Nonoperating Items (3)	(22)	–1.1%	13	0.6%	(27)	–1.1%
Reorganization (4)	(30)	–1.6%	(36)	–1.6%	(42)	–1.6%
Total	163	8.4%	214	9.6%	181	7.1%
Adjusted Pretax Profit	280	14.5%	316	14.2%	352	13.7%

(Exhibit continues)

Exhibit 11-1 (Continued)

Notes

1) a.	Eliminate excess owner's salary			
	Owners salary & bonus	281	300	311
	Fair market salary	(135)	(142)	(150)
	Subtotal	146	158	161
b.	Eliminate owner's excess perks including, travel & entertainment, automobile, and life insurance	34	49	38
c.	Eliminate owner related pension expense	18	30	30
	Total	198	237	229
2) a.	Eliminate nonrecurring bad debts related to the bankruptcy of one customer	0	0	21
b.	Eliminate burglary loses not reimbursed by insurance	13	0	0
c.	Eliminate the one time security system installation expenses	4	0	0
	Total	17	0	21
3)	Eliminate the following nonoperating items:			
	a. Interest expense	17	31	27
	b. Investment income	(15)	(18)	(22)
	c. Gain on the sale of fixed assets	(24)	13	(32)
	Total	(22)	13	(27)
4)	Adjust the financial statements from a real estate ownership situation to a leased facility situation			
	add: Fair market rent	62	68	74
	less: Depreciation	(32)	(32)	(32)
	Total	30	36	42

Any other payments the owner receives from the business should be reviewed. Rent payments, lease payments, or any other payments should be adjusted to what the business would pay in the open market.

When making adjustments keep in mind two key items. The first is that the adjusted income statement should present the profit situation of the company as if the company were being run to maximize profits, not minimize taxes. The second item is documentation. A buyer will want to verify every adjustment. Maintain good records of the adjustments and make the original source documents available for review.

Nonrecurring Income and Expense Adjustments

Nonrecurring income and expenses are those items which were incurred at some point in the past but are not anticipated in the future. They are unusual, nonrecurring, one-time items. An example of a nonrecurring item would be expenses related to a disaster such as a flood or fire. A second example would be an extraordinary bad debt caused by the unexpected bankruptcy of a major customer. A third example might be expenses related to a new advertising program that was initiated a few years ago but failed and was abandoned. Nonrecurring income and expense items are unique; only a thorough analysis of the recent history of the company will identify them.

When making adjustments for nonrecurring expense items, make sure that they are really *nonrecurring.* Buyers review them carefully. Also be sure to have good documentation supporting the amount of the adjustment.

Nonoperating Expense Adjustments

It is the profit producing assets which give value to an operating company. Income and expenses related to other assets such as investments, the cash value of life insurance, real estate, and other nonoperating items are not part of the ongoing operations. Therefore they are eliminated. The nonoperating assets and income should be handled separately from the sale of the ongoing company.

Interest expense is another nonoperating item. It is adjusted out because it relates to the capital structure of the company, not to the operations. A buyer's capital structure may be completely different than the company's current capital structure.

Organizational Change Adjustments

The fourth area of adjustment deals with organizational changes. It is often decided that the company will be sold under a different organizational structure than currently exists. The most common example of this is real estate. Frequently the owner of the company will want to sell the business but not the real estate, intending to rent the facility to the buyer for a future source of income. In this situation, an appropriate rent expense would be added to the expenses on the income statement and the historic depreciation expense of the building would be eliminated.

Other examples of organizational adjustments include leased machinery and rented or leased equipment, or perhaps a patent or copyright which the owner desires to retain.

Each restructuring adjustment is unique and needs to be handled separately. The adjustments should present the company as if the restructuring had occurred prior to the historic period analyzed. This allows the buyer to see the historic financial performance of the company under the same circumstances that will probably exist in the future.

BALANCE SHEET ADJUSTMENTS

When adjusting the balance sheet of the company your ultimate goal is a balance sheet that presents the current market value of the operating assets, operating liabilities, and owner's equity. It is necessary to adjust only the most recent balance sheet; other historic balance sheets needn't be adjusted. What is important is presenting the true economic picture of the assets as they exist today; a current picture that will show a buyer those assets and liabilities that will be included in the sale.

The basic steps to follow when adjusting are not hard to understand. The individual circumstances of a company, however, may include a complicated situation which requires substantial expertise and effort. The first step is to review the assets and liabilities of the company and determine which are operating and which are nonoperating. Once the nonoperating items are identified the seller needs to decide which of these assets are to be included in the sale. It is assumed that all of the operating assets are to be included. The items not to be included in the sale are eliminated from the balance sheet. Once this is done, the balance sheet lists only the items being included in the sale.

The next step is to identify the fair market value of the remaining items and adjust the original balance sheet figures as appropriate. Once the numbers are finalized and a new equity figure is calculated, this new number should represent the owner's true economic equity in the company. It should be noted that this equity relates only to the tangible assets of the company. It does not include goodwill or any other intangible items. An example of an adjusted balance sheet is presented in Exhibit 11–2.

Operating and Nonoperating Assets and Liabilities

An operating asset or liability is one that is an integral part of the normal day-to-day workings of the company. The most obvious items are inventory, fixed assets, accounts receivable, and trade accounts payable. Nonoperating assets are assets which are owned by the company but are not part of the day-to-day operations. Included in the nonoperating area are items such as investments, the owner's personal assets (car, boat, condominium, airplane, etc.), the cash value of officers' life insurance, accrued or prepaid income taxes, and debt.

All operating items should be included in the sale of the business, but the business owner has several choices with nonoperating items. The owner can transfer title and personally take possession of the items; the items can be sold separate from the business; or the items can be included in the sale of the business.

If you decide to include nonoperating assets in the sale, be careful. Make sure they enhance the price paid. If the buyer pays

Exhibit 11–2
Sample Company
Adjusted Balance Sheet
December 31, 19XX
($000)

ASSETS	Per Books	Adjustments		Adjusted
Current Assets				
Cash	19	0		19
Accounts Receivable	152	(10)	(1)	142
Inventory	78	0		78
Other Current Assets	86	(82)	(2)	4
Total Current Assets	335	(92)		243
Net Fixed Assets	66	19	(3)	85
Other Assets	7	(7)	(4)	0
Total Assets	408	(80)		328
LIABILITIES				
Current Liabilities				
Accounts Payable	11	0		11
Accrued Other Liab.	37	(30)	(5)	7
Notes Payable	11	(11)	(6)	0
Total Current Liabilities	59	(41)		18
Long-Term Liabilities	89	(89)	(6)	0
Total Liabilities	148	(130)		18
Owner's Equity	260	50		310
Total Liabilities & Equity	408	(80)		328

Exhibit 11-2 (Continued)

Notes

1) Increase the reserve for bad debts to state accounts receivable at their estimated net realizable value.

2) Eliminate nonoperating investments.

3) Eliminate the net book value of real estate ($44,000) and revalue the equipment to its fair market value ($63,000).

4) Eliminate the cash value of officers' life insurance.

5) Eliminate accrued income taxes.

6) Eliminate notes and loans payable (auto loan and real estate mortgage).

---

for only the operating value of the business when nonoperating items are included, he or she is getting the nonoperating assets for nothing. The seller receives no value for them. Let us examine some of the common items on a balance sheet and discuss their operating or nonoperating characteristics.

Cash is an operating asset. It is required to conduct normal day-to-day transactions; without it, bills cannot be paid. The important questions are, How much cash is necessary for the day-to-day operations of the company? and Does the company have excess cash? Excess cash is a nonoperating asset—it could be separated from the company without affecting the day-to-day operations or the profit produced by those operations.

Inventory and accounts receivable are operating assets. They usually make up the bulk of the working capital. They should always be included in the adjusted balance sheet.

Fixed assets are a mixed category. Most fixtures and equipment are important to the operations of the company, but there are usually several items that are nonoperating. These could include land and buildings (unless it is a special purpose facility), personal automobiles, airplanes or boats, real estate held for investment and other personal items. A proper analysis in this area requires that each item be examined on an individual basis and the appropriate determination made.

"Other assets" is a collection of items. Again determining whether an item in this category is operating or nonoperating must be done on an individual basis. Items such as utility or rent deposits or an investment in a purchasing cooperative are operating assets. Investments, officer notes receivable, and the cash value of life insurance are nonoperating.

On the liability side of the balance sheet, day-to-day debts such as accounts payable, accrued wages, and other similar items are operating. Other items are not. Income taxes should be eliminated from the adjusted balance sheet. An owner cannot assume that a buyer will take over the company's existing tax liabilities.

Loans, notes payable, and other formalized debt is a gray area. Debt is a capital structure decision and therefore nonoperating. However, buyers frequently assume the debt of the company.

You can successfully present the adjusted balance sheet to a buyer with or without the debt; however the most common presentation is without the debt. This is because a standard presentation is being prepared to be shown to many buyers. Some buyers will have lots of cash or will have their own sources of debt. They may not want to assume any of the existing debt. Other buyers may be struggling to come up with the down payment and will want to assume as much debt as they can.

The debt-free presentation is simple and easy to comprehend. It is also easy to adapt. One can take a debt-free situation and easily create and analyze several different debt scenarios. If your presentation includes debt, only one scenario is presented, and it may not meet the needs of the buyer.

If you decide to present a balance sheet with interest bearing debt included, it is important that the income statement presentation is consistent. If interest bearing debt is included on the balance sheet, the interest expense related to the debt must be included on the income statements.

Fair Market Value Adjustments

After the operating/nonoperating analysis is completed, and the items to be included in the sale have been identified, the fair market value of these items needs to be determined and adjustments made. The balance sheet prepared by an accountant values the assets of the company based on their original cost. Now that the business is being sold, the original cost is irrelevant—only the current fair market value is important. If the fair market value is different than the value shown on the balance sheet, an adjustment needs to be made.

Fair market value does not mean replacement value. It does not mean salvage value. It does not mean insurable value. The fair market value of an item is defined as the value in place of a similar item. A similar item is one of similar age that is in the same condition and has the same utility. It means the amount someone would pay if they located, purchased, and installed a similar item.

The fair market value of the inventory and accounts receivable should also be examined. If the company has obsolete inventory or inventory that has declined in value, the value of the inventory should be restated. If the company has inventory that has increased in value since it was purchased, the value should be increased. The accounts receivable of the company should also be decreased for any slow-paying or uncollectible accounts.

With the elimination of nonoperating items and the fair market value adjustments, the adjusted balance sheet is now complete and should be ready to be included in the selling documents.

Section 4
The Buyer

Chapter 12
Who Is the Buyer?

The buyer of a business can be almost anyone. It could be an individual looking for a business as an owner/operator, or perhaps a wealthy investor or group of investors looking for a good investment. Corporations, large and small, public and private, are probably the most prolific buyers. Foreign companies and investors are increasingly looking for a foothold in the United States. They are buying a significant number of American companies. Other potential buyers could be competitors, vendors, customers, or even the employees of the company.

The best buyers are those with experience! Why? Because those that have bought or sold a business before have gone through the process. They understand the transaction and are familiar with negotiations, documentation, and all of the other complexities of purchasing a business. It is really in the seller's best interest to seek a relationship with an experienced professional whose ability and fairness can be confirmed rather than relying on someone whose background is inadequate for buying, owning, and managing a business enterprise.

This chapter will present a brief discussion of each of the most common types of buyers. Their various motivations, weaknesses, and strengths will be addressed. Some buyers are easy to deal with; some are difficult. Some buyers have substantial resources; others do not. Recognizing some of the basic characteristics of cer-

147

tain types of buyers will help a seller identify which buyer will be easiest to deal with and will be most likely to meet the seller's needs and objectives.

A COMPETITOR

A seller considering potential buyers will usually consider competitors. A competitor may be a good choice for several reasons. A competitor knows the industry, and may also know the individual company. Most likely the competitor will look at the purchase as an opportunity to grow.

In spite of what appears to be good reasons to consider competitors as potential buyers, there are also several negative aspects to consider. While a buyout by a competitor can be successful, there also can be considerable risk for the seller.

Competitors are usually not experienced buyers. They do not understand what it takes to make a successful transaction. When selling to a competitor there can be significant overlap between the two companies, and probably no synergy. Because of this a competitor is likely to pay less for the business. Also, when dealing with a competitor it is very difficult to negotiate and educate the buyer about the business. The competitor will already have strong opinions about the seller's business. It will be very difficult to change any inaccurate opinions the competitor may have.

Perhaps the biggest risk to the seller is understood when you consider the question, what happens when the sale to a competitor falls through? The competitor has been given confidential and proprietary information about the company. He or she knows the company's secrets. Knowledge of this proprietary information may provide the competitor with a competitive advantage. Also, gossip may spread throughout the industry and community. Regardless of the facts, a number of bad rumors may be spread about the seller and the seller's company. Whether these rumors are true or not they could seriously affect the future operations of the company.

If the decision is made to try to sell the business to a competitor, approach the indirect competitors first—those that are in a different market area. If they decide to buy they will be looking at a real market expansion and there will be less overlap. Also, since they do not compete in the same primary market area, the risks associated with a failed transaction are not as great.

Before contacting any competitors learn as much as possible about them. It is most important to obtain copies of their credit reports. Determine if they can afford to purchase your company. Once you feel that you have adequate information, prioritize the possible buyers to determine who to contact first. In the initial discussions ask them how they would analyze an acquisition. Find out what their motivation is: Are they really interested in buying or are they just trying to get information about your company? Try to find out how they would assess value. It is important to determine within the first few meetings whether they are truly interested in buying and whether the possibility exists of a meeting of the minds on price and value.

A SUPPLIER OR VENDOR

A large supplier of materials to the company may be a potential buyer. The idea of having a captive user of their product may be desirable. However, the seller must again be careful—the risks and pitfalls of dealing with a vendor are the same as those encountered when dealing with a competitor.

When identifying vendors to approach as potential buyers, consider several things. Start with your largest and most important vendors. How important are you to that vendor? The more significant you are as a customer, the more interested the vendor will be. If the vendor is part of a larger organization, find out who the owner is. Does it have a history of acquiring related companies? If so, your chances are good; if not, it could be an uphill battle.

Once potential vendors are identified, follow the same process as with competitors. Learn as much about the vendors as possible. Prioritize to determine who will be contacted first. Get the information needed to determine the possibility of success in the first couple of meetings. If the vendor is not serious or you are miles apart, sever negotiations.

A CUSTOMER

A large customer may be a potential buyer. If the company's products are important to them, they may be interested in obtaining a supply they can control. However, when dealing with a customer, caution is advised. Some of the same problems that exist for a competitor or supplier arise. But also keep in mind that a customer who knows the company is for sale may begin to look for an alternate source for the products you provide.

The most promising prospect in this area would be a customer owned by a large public company. This is especially true if the parent company has a history of acquiring related companies.

When considering customers as potential buyers follow the same guidelines as with competitors or vendors. Investigate them thoroughly. Confirm their financial ability to purchase the company. Prioritize to determine who you will contact first. Determine the possibility of success in the first couple of meetings—if it doesn't exist, don't proceed.

SELLING TO EMPLOYEES

Every year many companies are purchased by employees. Federal laws encourage employee buyouts with specific tax incentives. It is a phenomenon which is becoming more and more popular. In the future the number of employee groups purchasing the companies they work for will probably increase.

Many of these purchases are structured as Employee Stock Ownership Trusts (ESOTS), which are trusts established to purchase and hold stock for employees. The Federal government has established significant tax incentives for purchases made through an ESOT.

In spite of this trend, a seller should be very careful about dealing with employees as potential buyers. Selling to employees is recommended only after dealings with other potential buyers have failed.

There are three good reasons for selling to employees. The first is goodwill. The seller will be perceived by both the workers and the community as a benevolent employer. He or she is sharing with the workers giving them a part of a company they helped to build and make successful. The second reason is the tax benefits which can be achieved if the stock is purchased by an ESOT. The third reason is availability. Employees are often available and ready to buy the business. Employees often feel they have the right to be considered as buyers. They know of the success of the business and want to participate in that success as owners.

Unfortunately, there are many reasons why sellers should not deal with employees as buyers except as a last resort. The first reason is that employees are employees—they are *not* entrepreneurs. They are not motivated to be business owners; if they were, they wouldn't be working for the seller. Employees are usually more risk averse than entrepreneurs, and they like the security of employment.

The seller who sells to employees is under additional obligation to make sure the deal is fair and workable. If the business does not do well after the transaction is completed, the employees may accuse the seller of overpricing the business or perhaps even fraudulent conveyance.

There are other risks for a seller negotiating with employees. The seller and employees are put in an adversarial relationship. If negotiations are difficult, the operations of the company may suffer. The seller also loses confidentiality. Information previously unavailable to employees will be disclosed. This could result in resentment on both sides.

Employees considering the purchase of a company will almost always ask for concessions from the seller. The first concession will be time: they will want time to arrange financing, time to put together a deal. Employees will almost always ask for special price and term considerations. They will expect the seller to give them a better deal than would be offered to other buyers.

If employees are given an opportunity to buy and they are not successful, other problems may arise. A failure can cause strained relationships between the owner and employees. As a result some employees may leave the company. Also, resentment may build against the eventual buyer—many employees will believe that *they*, not the successful buyer, should own the company.

The intent of this discussion is not to discourage sellers from considering employees as potential buyers of the company. This author believes that the current trend in employee purchases is good and should be continued. The intent is emphasized that the risks associated with selling to employees are great, and must be properly understood and addressed.

SELLING TO AN OWNER/OPERATOR

Often the most likely buyer of a small or medium-sized business is an owner/operator. Frequently a middle or senior level manager from another company will want to personally own and manage a company. These buyers generally have some money for a down payment, although it may not be much. This money often comes from a retirement fund, savings, or a second mortgage on a home.

An individual interested in buying the business may prove to be an excellent buyer, or a waste of time. Extra care must be taken in evaluating and qualifying these buyers. Careful consideration must be made to determine the strengths, weaknesses, and motivation of the buyer.

Owners/operators are usually very conservative about price. They are unwilling to pay a high price for the business for several reasons. First and foremost is that they cannot afford it. In a very real sense they are often putting everything they have into the business. If the business they purchase is not successful, they will lose everything. Furthermore, they will be very conservative about the future of the business. The value is more likely to be based on past performance than on future expectations.

The price and terms of the transaction will be such that the buyer will pay for the business over time. If funds cannot be borrowed against the assets of the business, then the buyer will ask the seller to carry the debt. The debt will be paid for out of the future profits of the business. If the business cannot support the level of debt, then the debt will not be paid.

THE INVESTMENT GROUP

This type of buyer is a group of one or more investors who have pooled their money together to purchase a business. They desire to own a business because they believe they can achieve a higher rate of return by owning a private company than with other investments.

Many different types of investor groups exist. Some consist of a few friends or business associates who join forces for one transaction. Others are specialists in an industry or a specific purchasing technique. These groups purchase companies that meet their investment criteria. The two most well known types of investment groups are leveraged buyout specialists and venture capitalists.

Leveraged buyout groups specialize in asset-intensive companies. Their technique is to fund the purchase price by borrowing against the assets. They will probably not be interested in the purchase unless it can be structured so that there is little or no out of pocket down payment. Before they decide to buy, they will develop a reasonable reorganization plan to restructure the company, the goal being a more efficient more profitable company. Inefficient assets often are sold off for cash. This allows the group to pay down the debt, resulting in a larger cash flow available as profit to the group.

Most venture capital groups are interested in start-up companies which have a technological or other market advantage and a good probability for rapid growth. They are usually not interested in an established, stable company. The exception being a company which does have a proprietary or other advantage which could be exploited and turned into rapid growth.

Investor groups consist of investors who are motivated by rates of return. They are price conscience. If historic earnings levels do not provide an adequate return, they will probably not be interested. They do not look at the business as anything other than an alternative investment opportunity.

Investment groups frequently do not desire or are not able to become involved in the day-to-day management of the company. The members of the group are involved as *investors*. While members of the group may have significant management experience, they often do not have particular expertise in the industry or the company's technology. They usually want to have professional managers run the business, and they often ask the existing owner to remain and manage the business.

Leverage is a key tool used by most investment groups. Leverage is often necessary to increase the rate of return to the level desired by members of the group. Thus, the more money that can be borrowed against the company, the more desirable it is to an investment group.

A PUBLIC CORPORATION

From the standpoint of price, a public company is usually the most desirable suitor. Due to their access to public equity markets and their size, they can often offer a price higher than many other buyers can afford. Also, due to their financial structure and their sources of debt, they often prefer to pay cash for the acquisition of small and medium-sized companies.

When dealing with a public company, start at the top. The Chief Executive Officer (CEO) is usually involved in all acquisitions. If it is more appropriate to deal with someone else, the CEO will refer you to the proper individual. Find out what the real level of interest is at the upper echelon. All too often a seller wastes valuable time and effort dealing with a lower level executive who does not have the authority to make a decision. Always deal with the person with authority.

Learn as much about the company and its key managers as possible. Large corporations often seem to be impersonal entities; however, acquisition decisions are made by the managers and executives. Find out about these people—they are the ones you will negotiate with. They will decide whether to pursue the acquisition.

Thanks to government reporting requirements, much information can be obtained about public companies. Obtain copies of recent annual reports. Securities and Exchange filings will also provide detail about operations and managements. 10-k reports often provide more operational and financial detail than annual reports. Proxy statements provide detail about current management. 8-Q statements provide information about any previous acquisitions the company has made.

Study this information. Learn what the strategies of the company are. Would your business fit within those strategies? Scrutinize the financial position of the company. Does it have the cash to make the purchase? What is the experience of the key managers and executives? Can you effectively deal with them?

A PRIVATE CORPORATION

Many large private corporations are involved actively in the acquisition of small and medium-sized companies. Many of these corporations have substantial resources and will pay premium prices for a business. Many small and medium-sized private corporations also have acquired companies, or seek to acquire them. These companies, as buyers, can be as desirable as public corporations.

The difficulty in dealing with a private company is that they are private. Financial information, corporate strategies, and other key information is not readily available. This puts the seller at a disadvantage in evaluating potential buyers.

A seller must carefully evaluate a closely held corporation as a potential buyer. Many companies are not as successful as they appear. Can they really afford to purchase the company? Is the personality of top management such that you can work well with them? Will your company fit in well with the existing operations and planned growth of the company? These are all important questions. During initial discussions the seller wants to find out as much about the buyer as the buyer wants to find out about the seller.

A FOREIGN BUYER

Foreign corporations and individuals are actively involved in acquiring companies in the U.S. market. Between 15 percent and 20 percent of all large and medium-sized corporate acquisitions in the United States are made by foreign buyers. Market conditions are such that there are advantages to both the foreign buyer and domestic seller.

Foreign buyers are often more motivated than domestic buyers, and consequently, will often pay a higher price. Foreign buyers desire entrance to U.S. business and equity markets. The United States remains the center of capitalism, and is considered a safe haven for business equity. Furthermore, foreign businesspeople often transfer assets to the United States for political reasons.

There are two other very significant reasons why foreign buyers will offer higher prices. The first relates to taxes, the second to rates of return. In many areas of the world, especially Europe, goodwill is a tax deductible expense. This is not the case in the United States. Thus, a foreign purchaser could have a tax advantage over a domestic buyer, which would allow the foreign buyer to pay more.

Prevailing rates of return in some areas of the world are substantially lower than in the United States. Because of this a foreign buyer valuing a business in the United States may use a lower required rate of return, resulting in a higher value and price for the business.

Dealing with foreign buyers is not difficult. There are no significant government restrictions on foreign ownership of U.S. industry. There are only minimal reporting requirements. However, it is strongly recommended that the seller's advisors, the intermediary and attorney, have experience in international acquisitions.

When dealing with a foreign buyer, take the time and effort to learn about the customs and traditions of the buyer. The personal relationship of the buyer and seller is of the utmost importance, in an international transaction. Let the buyer know that you are interested and cooperative. There is no better way to communicate this than through a knowledge of the buyer's country, customs, traditions, and business practices.

Chapter 13
Finding the Buyer

Finding potential buyers is often a difficult, frustrating job. For a quality business, the problem is not whether there are buyers out there but locating and contacting them. The market of buyers is fragmented and dispersed. The right buyer for your business may be just around the corner, or he or she may be located in a different state—perhaps even in a different country.

Given that the buyer could be anywhere, how does the seller find the buyer? Looking for the buyer can be like looking for the proverbial needle in the haystack.

Finding the buyer is one area where a good intermediary can be most helpful. A good intermediary will have developed a list of potential buyers; people and companies interested in buying. As the seller selects an intermediary, one of the most important things to analyze is the intermediary's ability to find interested buyers. Remember that anyone can place an ad in the classified section of the newspaper. The intermediary should be a member of the "network" through which a buyer can be found.

GEOGRAPHICALLY, WHERE IS THE BUYER?

When sellers think of prospective buyers, they often assume that the buyer will have the same geographic reference as the seller and the company. In other words, if the company is a local com-

157

pany it is most likely that the buyer will be local as well. If the company is regional then the buyer will come from the same region. This assumption is one of the biggest mistakes that can be made when looking for a buyer. More often than not, the best buyer for a company will come from a different area of the country or perhaps even from overseas.

A seller does not know where an interested buyer may come from, so the seller must make as complete an effort as possible. Buyers should be solicited locally, regionally, nationally, and internationally. The more potential buyers that are aware of the company, the more interested parties there will be and the better the seller's chances of having a successful sale with the best price and terms possible.

There is a rule of thumb that can generally be followed regarding the geographic location of the buyer. The rule is that the larger and the more unique the business, the greater the chances that the buyer will not be local. Conversely, if the business is small and not unique—if there are many businesses like it—the less likely it is that the buyer will be from out of town. It should be remembered that this rule of thumb is not hard and fast. There are a significant number of exceptions to the rule. It provides only a general trend.

IDENTIFYING POTENTIAL BUYERS

The most effective way of finding a buyer is to identify through some screening process those people or companies with an interest in purchasing the company and then contacting the appropriate parties directly. The hard part is making up a complete list of those that may be interested.

Some intermediaries maintain a list of buyer's that have purchased businesses in the past. Many of these buyers purchase companies on an ongoing basis. Buyers which have purchased companies within your industry or in a similar industry may be good potential buyers.

Most companies receive occasional inquiries from parties interested in purchasing them. Those that have expressed interest in the past are known, and would be likely candidates.

Another way to identify potential buyers is to think of the sale as a merger. Would your company make a good fit and be compatible with another company? Who are the other companies? An effort should be made to identify as many as possible.

The seller should also identify similar companies which are not direct competitors, such as companies in an affiliated industry. Perhaps companies that use similar sales and marketing efforts, manufacturing processes or technology. It could be any company that is similar enough to provide some synergy or economies from a merger of the two companies.

The seller should also identify competitors or others in the industry that have been purchased during the past few years. Those buyers that have acquired in the past may be interested in doing so again. Also, try to find out what other suitors were involved. Perhaps the fact that they lost out on the previous acquisition will make them more determined to acquire the next opportunity.

Identify the types of companies that have acquired other companies in the industry. Perhaps there are companies similar to those that have made acquisitions that would be good potential buyers. If a competitor was purchased by a company in a different industry, maybe other members of that same industry would be interested in purchasing your company. If the acquisition of the competitor was based on sound business judgment, then other similar companies may be interested in acquiring your company for the same reasons.

Industry and trade associations are good sources of interested buyers. People at these organizations are often aware of what companies in the industry have been acquired and by whom. They are also aware of parties interested in acquiring a company in the industry. It is common practice for interested buyers to contact the association to obtain industry information and learn about companies in the industry.

Once a list of specific individuals and companies is developed, a letter and a copy of the company summary should be sent to everyone on it. The letter should explain that the company described in the company summary is for sale. It should provide the name, address, and phone number of the contact person. The letter should also state that additional information will be provided to interested parties once a confidentiality agreement is signed and a buyer information sheet completed. The contact person may wish to follow up each letter with a phone call.

CLASSIFIED ADVERTISEMENTS

Classified advertising in trade journals and business or regional newspapers is often an effective way of finding potential buyers. Trade journals, in particular, allow a seller to address a very specific market of potential buyers.

Classified advertisements should be blind ads. The identity of the company should be omitted for confidentiality. The ad should specify that a company is for sale. It should identify the industry and the general regional location of the company, and present some basic company data such as sales volume, profitability, or other information of general interest to a buyer. The ad should then ask interested parties to respond to a post office box or other blind address. Interested buyers are also requested to include references and other pertinent information with their response. Those that respond to the classified ad are sent the company summary, confidentiality agreement, and buyer information sheet.

Trade Journals

Trade journals provide an effective medium through which to advertise your business. A trade journal ad allows the seller to target a specific market; a classified ad placed in the appropriate trade journals has a good chance of being seen by those companies and individuals that are familiar with your industry. Trade journal ads often are seen by people who do not regularly read business opportunity ads in daily newspapers.

Newspaper Advertisements

A classified ad in the business opportunities section of the newspaper is another effective way of advertising. These sections are seen by many people interested in acquiring a business. However, this audience, unlike the trade journal audience, is not focused. The seller may therefore receive many responses from unqualified buyers. More effort may be required to qualify buyers located through business opportunity classified ads.

Advertisements should be placed in appropriate regional or national newspapers. Each paper usually has certain preferred editions for business opportunity ads, usually the Sunday edition. Experienced corporate and individual buyers frequently read these sections looking for potential acquisition candidates. Regional and national newspapers will provide substantially more exposure than local newspapers. Local newspapers are most appropriate when the business has appeal to a specific type of local buyer.

WORD OF MOUTH

Buyers also are located by way of "word of mouth." Word of mouth can be very effective; however, when word is out on the street, all confidentiality is lost.

Suppliers, trade association personnel, and others in the industry are in constant contact with people involved in the industry. They can often find an interested party. Trade associations frequently maintain lists of companies in the industry that are for sale. They provide information about these companies to interested buyers.

The major and perhaps fatal weakness of using word of mouth is confidentiality. Open knowledge of the sale can be damaging to the business. Once competitors, suppliers, and customers find out that the business is for sale, anything can happen. Sellers should exercise caution using this method to find buyers. In fact, it should be used only as a last resort.

Chapter 14

Dealing with the Buyer

The difference between a successful sale and failure often depends on how effectively the buyer and seller deal with each other. As all buyers are different, there are no set rules on how to deal with them. There are however many general rules which may apply, which this chapter addresses.

This chapter also includes a detailed discussion of what is needed to determine whether a buyer is qualified, financially and otherwise, to purchase the business.

The final section of this chapter addresses the confidentiality agreement. A list of items to be included in the agreement is presented.

KNOW THE BUYER

To deal most effectively with the buyer, the seller and the negotiator must learn as much about the buyer as possible. Find out where the buyer went to school, what experience he or she has, what his or her areas of expertise, personal interests, and hobbies are. Look into their families, their major accomplishments, their political or religious backgrounds. In addition to learning about the buyer, familiarize yourself with any special customs or traditions of the buyer. This is especially pertinent in the case of a foreign buyer.

163

The more you learn about a person, the better you can understand and deal with that person as a buyer. Detailed knowledge is necessary in order to develop the personal relationship that is so helpful during the sales process.

BUYER/SELLER CHEMISTRY

The "chemistry" or relationship that develops between a buyer and a seller is very important to the success of the transaction. Frequently, negotiations deal with numbers, documents, and hard assets, and the personal relationship between the buyer and seller is neglected. The "chemistry" of the transaction deals with the people, and it is most important. When you get down to the real issues, it is people that make the company successful.

The seller and buyer need to make a special effort to establish a personal relationship and mutual respect for each other. Many of the early discussions will include talk about personal things. Such conversation is necessary to develop the proper relationship between the two parties.

Buying or selling is more than a rational process—it is an emotional process. If the buyer and the seller can develop the proper relationship, then the negotiations will be smoother and the sale will be much easier to consummate.

The seller makes an emotional commitment when he or she concludes that "I can sell my business to this buyer. The buyer is important to me and I can trust that he or she will take good care of it." The buyer makes a similar commitment when he or she concludes that "I can buy (trust) a business that this seller has created and managed. The seller is an important person to me and I can trust him or her." The successful relationship occurs when both parties care about each other as well as the company.

One critical topic that must be addressed during the development of this relationship is the future role of the owner. Both parties must be sensitive to the needs of the other. Care must be taken to establish a future role that fits everyone's goals.

Chemistry involves not only the issues of the buyer and seller, but the issues of the employees as well. It is the buyer's and seller's mutual responsibility to develop the proper relationship one which benefits all parties. And take care not to let the intermediary/negotiator become a barrier between you and the buyer. Your own personal time and effort must be spent to develop the proper rapport.

MOTIVES FOR BUYING

Understanding the goals, objectives, and motives of a buyer is an important step in the selling process. Such an understanding is essential to effective negotiations. The seller should recognize that the buyer is often interested in the company for reasons not obvious to the seller. The buyer rarely buys what the seller thinks he or she is selling.

The buyer typically has very specific reasons for purchasing a company. Those reasons may be part of a much larger business plan or they may involve only the success of the one company. A company may have many strengths and desirable characteristics. What is most valuable to the buyer is often different than what is most valuable to the seller.

The following is a list of some of the most common motives for acquiring a firm:

1. To achieve growth.
2. To obtain a new product line.
3. To avoid the risks of internal expansion.
4. To reduce competition.
5. To increase profits and cash flow.
6. To acquire a larger market share or a more dominant market position.
7. To expand geographically.
8. To diversify.
9. To offset the seasonality of existing operations.
10. To enhance the power, prestige, or ego of the company's owner or management.

11. To acquire a patent, technology, or research and development capabilities.

12. To acquire management expertise.

13. To gain access to the client list.

14. To cheaply acquire existing assets (rather than building new ones).

15. To move money out of a foreign country and into the United States.

16. To acquire a good investment opportunity.

BUYER QUALIFICATION

Discussions about buyer qualification usually center around the financial capabilities of the buyer. However, buyer qualification really should consider four areas in detail: financial resources, management expertise, technical expertise, and personality.

In the area of finance the pertinent question is, "Is the buyer financially able to purchase the company?" In the area of management the question is, "Does the buyer have the management experience and expertise necessary to manage the company after it is sold?" In the area of technical expertise the question is, "Does the buyer have the training, intellect, and experience necessary to understand the technology of the company?" In the area of personality the questions are, "Does the buyer have the people skills required to deal with the company's employees?" and "Does the buyer's personality fit well with the personality of the company and the seller?"

To answer the questions above the seller relies on information and documents from several sources. The documents required include personal financial statements or company financial statements. The statements should be detailed and offer enough history to make an assessment of the buyer's financial position and borrowing power. The seller should also try to obtain credit reports on the buyer to find out about the buyer's credit rating and past credit history. A personal resume of the buyer will provide insight about experience, management abilities, and technical expertise.

The seller should also ask the buyer for business or professional references, personal references, and financial references. It is important to follow up by contacting all of the references. Nobody can better assess a buyer than someone who has dealt with him or her in the past. The one catch about references is that they are provided by the buyer. It is unlikely that the buyer will provide the name of someone that will not provide a good reference. One way to get around this is to ask the references if they are aware of others who have dealt with the buyer. They may provide you with additional names of people not necessarily favored by the buyer. An interview with these people should provide a less biased opinion of the buyer.

During early discussions with the buyer find out what other companies the buyer has purchased. Talk to the former owners of these companies. They should be able to provide excellent insight about the buyer. Also, during your discussions with the buyer, find out as much as possible about the buyer's motives, needs, and objectives. Carefully access whether these motives and objectives are consistent with the resources of the company and the needs of the seller.

CONFIDENTIALITY

One of the hardest tasks, and biggest risks, of selling is providing confidential and proprietary information about the company. This information, if put in the wrong hands or if used for purposes other than analyzing an acquisition, could be damaging to the future operations of the company.

In an attempt to minimize and control this risk, the seller should require that all potential buyers sign a confidentiality agreement. This agreement should be a formal document. It should stress the importance and value of the information disclosed. It should define clearly the proper use of the information, and it should specify procedures or claims for violation of the agreement. This document lets the buyer know that the seller is intent on protecting the confidentiality of the company and will not tolerate anything less than complete confidentiality.

Listed below are several items which should be included in the confidentiality agreement.

1. The names and addresses of all parties.
2. A list of confidential documents provided to the prospective buyer.
3. A statement that the documents contain sensitive, proprietary, and confidential information.
4. A statement that the undersigned agrees that the information is sensitive, proprietary, and confidential.
5. A statement that the information will be held confidential and will not be disclosed to anyone.
6. A statement that the information is to be used only for the purposes of considering the acquisition and for no other purpose.
7. A statement that the agents, attorneys, accountants, and advisors of the buyer may review, and have access to, the information but they must agree to abide by the terms and conditions of the confidentiality agreement.
8. A statement that no copies or abstracts of the information will be made.
9. A statement that upon request, all of the documents provided will be returned to the seller.
10. A statement that the buyer is not obligated to hold any general publicly available information confidential.
11. A statement of the rights of the seller (including injunctive relief) in the event that the buyer violates this agreement.

While it is possible for a seller to write a confidentiality agreement, it is suggested that an attorney be consulted in order to assure that all the rights of the seller are protected.

Section 5
The Sale

Chapter 15
Negotiating

Negotiation is a potentially adversarial activity where the buyer and the seller attempt to reach a compromise that will reasonably satisfy the needs of both parties. In the area of mergers and acquisition, negotiations center around the price and terms. While price and terms are important both the buyer and the seller have other reasons for being involved in the transaction. They both have needs and objectives which a successful sale and purchase will help fulfill. The most successful negotiators can identify the non-monetary needs of the buyer and seller and satisfy them as part of the transaction. Sensitivity to all of the needs of the buyer and the seller is a very important part of a successful negotiation.

There is no set way to negotiate. No two companies, sellers, buyers, or deals are alike. The personality and circumstances of the parties involved greatly affect the negotiating strategy.

Negotiations take place between human beings, each with their own unique set of needs and objectives. A transaction will never be consummated unless the needs of both the buyer and seller can be satisfied. The negotiator must be able to analyze objectively the company being acquired as well as the needs of both parties. Once the negotiator understands these items, a deal structure must be developed that will meet the needs and be within the resources of all parties.

Negotiation is an art. There is no way to adequately discuss negotiation in a single chapter. Volumes have been written on the subject and many excellent professionals devote their careers to practicing it. This is one area in which every business owner, no matter how experienced or knowledgeable, should seek assistance.

This chapter presents several different ideas about negotiating the sale of a business. Not all of the ideas are applicable or appropriate in every situation. The business owner should determine which ideas can best be applied to the unique situations encountered by his or her company.

INTEGRITY AND CANDOR

Participants in the mergers-and-acquisitions industry rely upon the honesty and candor of their associates. The integrity of the parties involved is what makes the deal work. Those who are not honest, those who deceive, will fail. The workings of a business of any size are detailed and complicated. The sales transaction with its financing, tax effects, contracts, and other documents, is also complex. It is simply impossible to completely protect oneself. Thus, the buyer and seller both must rely on the integrity and good faith of the other party. There is no substitute for trust. Refuse to deal with any parties you perceive as untrustworthy.

PROBLEMS

Problems will arise throughout the negotiations—they are part of every transaction. Some problems can be anticipated, some cannot. If a company's weaknesses are known, one can anticipate differences of opinion regarding the significance of each weakness. There will be other unforeseen concerns and demands from the buyer as well.

The seller needs to be ready for unexpected problems. Persistence is necessary. Don't let the problems irritate you; be patient. Aggressively pursue creative solutions. It will be a plus if the buyer is experienced, one who has gone through the process before. He or she will know that problems will arise and must be dealt with.

KEEP IT SIMPLE

The old acronym, KISS (Keep It Simple Stupid) has a special application to mergers and acquisitions. Usually, the simplest way is the best way. Don't try to overcomplicate things. The more complicated the deal becomes, the more decisions a buyer or seller must make. As the number of decisions increases, the likelihood of a broken deal increases. People will abandon what they don't understand, especially when their own money is involved.

Some degree of complication is often inevitable, often due to the tax situation or the financing arrangements. It is important to take advantage of whatever tax or financing arrangements are beneficial; however, a transaction that is simple, straightforward, and easy to achieve has a greater chance of success.

WIN-WIN NEGOTIATING

There are two basic philosophies of negotiation. One is the win-lose philosophy. This is a competitive approach: one side tries to take advantage of the other side. The other approach is called the win-win philosophy. This philosophy emphasizes collaboration and compromise. The problem at hand, not the other party, is the enemy. Through creative compromise, a solution can be found which benefits both parties.

When buying or selling a business, the only negotiating philosophy that should be used is the win-win philosophy. There are many sensible business reasons why the win-lose philosophy should be avoided. For the purchase of the business to be most successful, the buyer and seller need to have a good relationship during the sales process and throughout the transition period. The win-lose philosophy requires that one party be at a disadvantage, thus making a decent ongoing relationship impossible.

For the sale to be successful, both parties must benefit. The seller must receive a fair price and the buyer must receive a sound investment. If the negotiations and transaction are based on a win-lose philosophy, the chances of failure increase dramatically. Even if the deal is successfully completed, it is more likely to fall apart at some later date and end up in court.

THE AUCTION METHOD OF NEGOTIATING

The auction method has existed since mankind began selling things. It has been used in the mergers-and-acquisition industry for decades. The auction method is easy to understand. The seller creates a situation where multiple buyers are trying to buy the company. These buyers bid against each other and the buyer who makes the most desirable offer purchases the company. The auction method is clearly the best from the seller's perspective—it results in the highest possible price and the best possible terms. However, making the auction method work is not easy. It requires hard work, good planning, effective negotiating, and some good luck.

The auction method almost always results in the highest possible price. Buyers participating in an auction are in a competitive situation. They not only want to buy the business, they want to beat the other buyers. Egos and emotions get involved. The buyer's motivation increases, and he or she is therefore willing to pay more for the business.

The success that a seller can expect from the auction method depends largely upon the law of supply and demand, whether it is a buyer's market or a seller's market. Fortunately for the seller, the mergers-and-acquisition market is usually a seller's market. Good companies are hard to find. There are almost always more buyers than sellers. A seller with a successful company can almost always make the auction method work.

Unfortunately, the auction method is not always effective. The seller may find that there are not several buyers interested in buying the business. If this is the case, then the seller must negotiate with individual buyers as they arise in an effort to obtain the best deal possible.

The three most critical steps required to make the auction method work are: 1) find several interested buyers; 2) control the timetable of the sales process; and 3) establish the rules and guidelines of the auction. If these three steps are handled successfully, chances are that the auction method will be successful.

The Number of Buyers

An auction requires two or more buyers. Sometimes it is difficult to find one, let alone two or more, interested buyers. The more interested buyers you identify and contact, the greater your chances of success. If you are considering using an intermediary to sell the business, one of the most important qualifications to assess is the intermediary's knowledge of and access to specific buyers who may be interested in the company.

The buyer must not only be interested but also impressed enough to want to buy. For this to occur the seller needs to have a business that is a good value as well as the sales and marketing ability to convince the buyer of that value.

Timing

It is often said that "timing is everything," and the auction method is no exception. The seller must control and influence the buyers so that they are ready to make an offer simultaneously. It doesn't help the seller if one buyer is just starting to analyze the company when another buyer is ready to make an offer.

To control the timing, the seller must control the sales process. The sales procedures must be fairly rigid. Different buyers must be influenced to proceed through the sales process at about the same pace. If they proceed at the same pace, they should be ready to purchase at about the same time.

The seller controls the pace of the buyers by setting and adhering to specific time guidelines. Initially, all the potential buyers must be contacted at the same time. Care should be taken to assure that the buyers all receive their sales literature at about the same time. Then there follows a period for analysis and questions. This period should be long enough for all the buyers to perform their needed analysis. The seller needs to check frequently that the buyer will be ready when it is time for the facility tours.

Inform the buyers that the facilities will be available for tours during a specified period. Exceptions to this schedule will only be allowed for extenuating circumstances. After the tours there is a second, but shorter, period for analysis, questions, and negotiation. After this the buyers should be ready to make an offer. Inform the buyers that offers will be accepted during a specific time period and that at the end of the period the best offer will be accepted.

Establish the Rules

In order for the auction method to succeed, everyone participating needs to know and understand the rules. Early in the process the seller needs to establish how the auction will be run and inform the buyers of the rules. Once the rules are established, they need to be enforced very strictly.

After simultaneously contacting all potential buyers, ask them to respond to the company summary within a specified period of time. At the end of this period the detailed business analysis and other sales literature is provided to all interested parties. After the interested parties have had time to review the DBA they are contacted to determine their level of interest. If several buyers are interested, then an auction can be pursued. At this time the rules are drawn up and provided to each interested buyer. (If too few buyers have shown interest to warrant using the auction method, another sales strategy can be implemented.)

The rules of the auction method should establish the timetable, when the facility tours will be held, when the seller will be available to meet with the buyer, and when the offers should be made. The rules should also establish upfront how the offers will be analyzed and how the seller will select the best offer. The seller has several options. Will there be only one opportunity to bid and the best offer will win? Will the seller select the best two or three offers and then have a second auction with only those buyers? Will the seller select the best two offers and then negotiate with them?

What is important is that a specific method for analyzing offers and negotiating be identified, and that the selected method, whatever it is, be followed. If the seller does not follow this method or changes the rules in the middle of the game, it will only anger the buyers. Some may walk away. Those that don't will look less favorably on the seller and the company.

LOWERING THE PRICE OR EASING THE TERMS

Sometime during the negotiation process a buyer will try to lower the price of the company or liberalize the terms of the transaction. Even in an auction situation a buyer will identify and emphasize weaknesses of the company. This is done in an effort to reduce the seller's expectations.

Every buyer will try to lower the price. Many do it because they want to get the best deal possible; others to feed their egos. Regardless of how good the deal is, they must try to put their mark on it.

A good negotiator anticipates the buyer's arguments, and is ready with answers. The negotiator will be able to either answer the concerns or explain how they have already been considered and included in the makeup of the transaction.

The buyer's presentation will be based on one of two arguments. The first and most common argument is that the company is not as good as the seller believes it is. The buyer will identify weaknesses and explain why they lower the value of the business. The second argument does not deal with the company but with the buyer and the market. It is that the buyer cannot afford to pay the price. Perhaps interest rates are too high or the buyer cannot borrow as much as he or she would like. Perhaps a source of financing is no longer available. The buyer will explain these or other problems and then ask for a concession in either price or terms.

Presented below is a list of common reasons used by buyers to convince the seller to lower the price. The seller and negotiator should be familiar with these reasons and be prepared to respond if the buyer raises them.

1. Possible problems with the accounts receivable.
2. Obsolete, unusable, or damaged inventory.

3. Excess or slow moving inventory.

4. Tax liabilities in excess of reserves.

5. Undisclosed company liabilities.

6. The liability of pending or possible litigation.

7. Potential product liability.

8. Uninsured company risks.

9. Unfunded pension costs.

10. The buyer will ask the seller pay accrued employee benefit costs up to the date of closing.

11. Excessive costs are required to repair or maintain the company's equipment.

12. Rising interest rates.

13. Government regulatory concerns.

14. Increased competition.

15. Tighter pricing by competition.

16. The future projections are aggressive and risky.

17. Concerns about the economy and the possibility of a recession.

18. The buyer can't afford to pay for a lot of goodwill.

19. The buyer needs money for working capital.

20. The buyer can't borrow as much against the business as desired.

The buyer also may attempt to reduce the price by requiring a very long escrow or requiring that a large amount of the purchase price be retained by the buyer as a reserve against a possible breach of representations and warranties.

Buyers are very creative; they will come up with many different reasons to lower the price. The seller who can anticipate these arguments and rightfully counter that they have already been considered or are not valid will be rewarded with the best price.

WHO WILL NEGOTIATE?

One of the most important decisions a seller makes is selecting a negotiator. The negotiator is the key player. The skills, knowledge, and preparation of the negotiator greatly affect the success of the transaction.

The person selected as the negotiator should have several characteristics. He or she should:

- not be emotionally involved in the sale;
- have an excellent knowledge of the company;
- understand the seller and the seller's goals and objectives;
- understand the buyer and the buyer's goals, desires and resources;
- have experience and skill in negotiating;
- be adept at presenting information in a way that favors the sellers position;
- be persuasive;
- be someone the buyer will trust;
- have knowledge and experience in mergers and acquisitions;
- be creative; and
- be able to come up with ways of meeting the needs of both the buyer and seller.

It is recommended that the seller not act as the negotiator. The emotional involvement of the seller in the company, as well as the seller's personal interest in the sale, make it very difficult for the seller to function effectively as a negotiator. A professional negotiator should be retained by the seller. This person can be the intermediary, or an attorney, or perhaps a professional negotiator. It should be someone the seller trusts and someone who possesses the needed skill, experience, and expertise.

THE FLOOR-CEILING PRINCIPLE

One of the basic rules of negotiating is to let the other party be the first to mention price. This is because the party that mentions price first, in effect, loses. This is called the floor-ceiling principle.

If the seller mentions price first, the amount stated by the seller establishes a ceiling. The buyer will start at the stated price and begin to negotiate downward. If the buyer mentions price first, that amount establishes a floor. The seller will start at this floor and begin to negotiate for a higher price.

The better negotiator is the one who influences the other party to state price first. One reason the auction method is so desirable is that it not only forces the buyer to mention price first, but also it forces the buyer to offer a high price because of the competition from other buyers.

THE NEGOTIATING MEETING

There are a number of things a negotiator can do to make a meeting with the buyer successful. The negotiating meeting is the negotiators arena. The negotiator should always be in control. The business owner, attorney, or accountant may be present, but they should participate only under the direction of the negotiator.

There should always be an agenda for the meeting. All present should have a copy and it should be followed. Make sure everyone is on time and that the meeting begin promptly. The best time for a meeting is in the morning, usually ten or eleven o'clock. The worst time for a meeting is in the early afternoon at one or two o'clock.

Take good notes. Periodically throughout the meeting, and especially at the end of the meeting, you should summarize what has been discussed. It is important to assure that everyone agrees on what has been decided and accomplished.

Whenever possible, use documentation. It is preferable to answer a question with a document. The buyer will be able to take the document and refer to it later. Make sure that the documentation used in the meeting is professional. It should have a table of contents and page numbers for easy reference.

Always begin the meeting by giving something, never by demanding something. Make a concession—this tells the buyer that you are acting in good faith. It also sets the stage for a meeting of mutually beneficial compromises and reduces the chances of the buyer making unreasonable demands.

Tell secretaries, staff people, and others that there are to be no interruptions or phone calls. If necessary, hold the meeting in a place where these hindrances will not be a problem.

Occasionally the buyer or a member of the buyer's team may arrive after the meeting has begun. He or she will request a briefing from the negotiator. However, rather than having the negotiator repeat what has been said, ask someone from the buyer's team to do it. This person, repeating the negotiator's presentation, becomes an advocate for the seller. In an effort to please the new arrival, he or she will be as complete and favorable as possible. If the presentation is incomplete, the negotiator can fill in the holes later.

As with any meeting with the buyer, appearance is important. The negotiator and the seller should look their best, as accomplished professionals. If the negotiation session is an important one where key issues are to be discussed, it may be advisable to hold a practice meeting, a mock session. This allows the negotiator the chance to preview potential questions and to better understand the position of the buyer.

PREPARATION

Though preparation is a definite advantage in negotiations. The negotiator needs to know the seller, the buyer, the company, and the current market situation. Adequate preparation will allow the negotiator to anticipate questions and provide adequate answers. Often a potentially damaging piece of information can be turned into an advantage.

Consider the arena where freedom and fortune are on the line—the courtroom. The skills of the attorney are critical. The quality of witnesses is important. But the most important factor is preparation. In the courtroom, the one who most often prevails is the one that is the most prepared. Likewise, in negotiating the purchase or sale of a business, the party that is best prepared will walk away with the most advantageous deal.

ATTENTION TO DETAIL

The aphorism, "that by small and simple things are great things brought to pass," often holds true in the complicated world of mergers and acquisitions. The seller's attention to detail as well as the continued accuracy and completeness of the documents and information provided to the buyer will go a long way in helping to finalize the transaction.

Over the weeks or months of dealing with the buyer countless documents and figures will be provided. Thousands of questions will be asked and answered. Through this series of contacts the buyer will develop opinions about the seller and the company. Insignificant errors, small contradictions, and incomplete answers may have an adverse effect on the buyer. The buyer's opinion of the seller's credibility is affected by the seller's attention to detail. The amount of trust the buyer has in the seller's documents depends on the amount of detail used in the preparation of those documents.

Attending to details helps prevent problems and pitfalls that might otherwise frustrate the transaction. Your command of details will help the transaction flow smoothly, with as few complications as possible.

Chapter 16
Structuring the Sale

Deal structuring is more often referred to as "the terms of the deal." The deal structure defines how and when the seller will be paid. Obtaining a deal structure that meets the needs of the seller is just as important as getting the desired price for the business. It is often said that the seller can set the price as long as the buyer can set the terms.

Understanding deal structuring, the different methods of payment and their associated risks, is necessary before the best deal structure can be determined. The best structure will meet both the needs of the seller and the objectives of the buyer. It will maximize value to the seller while making the business a good investment for the buyer.

The structure of the sale deals with three major items. These include 1) the amount of the payments; 2) the timing of the payments; and 3) in what form the payments will be made. Other parts of the deal structure include the security or collateral on future payments, any interest that will be paid, and any performance requirements of the seller relating to employment contracts, consulting contracts, noncompete agreements, or other forms of payment.

DEAL STRUCTURING METHODS

There are seven basic deal structuring methods, or forms of pay-ment: cash, notes payable, payments of stock, an earn out, a cove-nant not to compete, an employment contract, and a consulting contract. Some of these methods can be used individually. Others, such as the covenants and contracts, are usually used in combina-tion with one or more of the other methods. In addition to these seven there are other, more creative, forms of deal structuring which are occasionally used and which are usually more risky. Some of these methods are discussed in Chapter 17, "Creative Fi-nancing."

Cash

This is the method of payment that is most easily understood. The full payment of the purchase price is made in cash when the sales transaction is finalized.

Notes Payable

The seller of the business is asked by the buyer to carry back a note for part of the purchase price. This is a legally binding prom-ise made by the buyer to pay the seller the amount of the note plus interest at some future date. The timing of the payments and the rate of interest is negotiated between the buyer and the seller. A note payable may or may not have collateral. It may or may not be personally guaranteed by the buyer. In all cases, if the note re-lates to the purchase of the business, it should be secured by the assets of the business. Usually when the note to the seller is se-cured by the assets of the business, the note is subordinated to the other secured debts of the company.

Stock

This is a payment in kind for the business. A purchase for stock is most common when the buyer is a public company. A purchase with stock may or may not be equivalent to a cash purchase. It depends on the marketability of the stock, any sales costs related to selling the stock, whether selling the stock will effect the sales price, and whether any restrictive covenants exist.

The most important thing to remember when considering a payment in stock is that you are trading an investment in your own company for an investment in the acquiring company. Before, your success or failure depended on your ability to run your company; now your success, failure, and fortune depends on the vagaries of the stock market and the abilities of the management of the acquiring company. Do you, as the seller, want your fortune invested in the acquiring company? What would you do if the value of the acquiring company's stock fell significantly?

If a payment of stock is offered, the first question to ask is, "Is the stock marketable?" Can the stock be sold in the public markets? If the stock is not readily marketable, then there must be other good reasons to accept it as payment.

Stock that is not marketable is often used in the merger of two private companies. The seller usually becomes an employee of the merged companies and may become an officer or member of the board of directors.

Also consider the commissions which must be paid when the stock is sold. If a large block of stock is involved, commissions could be substantial.

One must also determine if selling the stock will affect its market price. Sometimes an attempt to sell the entire block of stock in a public market will have a negative effect on its price. Thus, the seller will usually sell the stock in small amounts over an extended period of time. If during this period the price of the stock increases, the seller could make a nice profit. However, if the price of the stock decreases, the seller could suffer substantial losses.

When stock is used as payment for the purchase of a business, the buyer may place some restrictive covenants on the stock. The most common restrictive covenant limits the seller's ability to sell the stock. The restrictive covenant may state that the seller cannot sell any stock for a period of time or that the seller cannot sell more than a certain amount of the stock within a specific time period. The buyer requires a restrictive covenant to eliminate the possibility of a decline in stock price if the seller were to sell all of the stock at once.

The negative effects of a restrictive covenant on a seller are obvious. Since the stock cannot be converted to cash for some time, the real value of the stock declines. The seller's fortune is now tied to the increases and decreases in the stock value of the acquiring company. A rise in the stock price could bring the seller a lot more than just the purchase price of his company. A decline in the stock price, however, could be devastating.

The seller can protect the stock from restrictive covenants. To guard against a decline in stock value it is often possible to purchase stock price insurance or to sell the stock short.

Earn Out

An earn out is a contingent payment. It is the buyer's promise to pay cash at some time in the future based on the achievement of specified objectives. It is like a performance bonus. The timing of the payments are negotiated and established in the earn out agreement. The amount of the payment is contingent on meeting the specific goals and objectives set forth in the agreement.

Earn outs are often tied to growth in revenue, profits, or both. They are often structured so that the seller is paid a percentage of the increased profits or a specified amount if the company achieves a predetermined revenue or profit level.

Earn outs only make sense if the seller wants to stay with the company during the earn out period and the seller has a good deal of confidence that the operating performance goals set forth in the earn out agreement can be achieved.

An earn out requires the purchased business to have separate records from the acquiring company. Be careful if the earn out is structured as a bonus—if substantial sums are involved, it could trigger unreasonable compensation claims by the Internal Revenue Service.

What is the earn out to be based on? Is it earnings, revenue, or some other measure? It is important that it is based on something over which the seller has control, something which is easily identified and measured and something which cannot be easily distorted or misstated.

An earn out is a complicated arrangement. If an earn out is being seriously considered, be sure to seek good counsel from someone who has experience and expertise in earn out agreements.

Covenant Not to Compete

Under a covenant not to compete the seller is paid for agreeing not to compete with the buyer. It is a legal and binding contract between the two parties. Sometimes the covenant payment is included as part of the down payment or note. More often it is a separate payment made to the seller monthly, quarterly, or annually, just like a salary. Covenants not to compete must be reasonable—a buyer must not make unrealistic demands on the seller. The covenant should address four areas. The first is the length of the covenant. The buyer should require only that the seller not compete for a reasonable amount of time, usually two or three years. The second item is the geographic area in which the seller cannot compete. The covenant should cover only the company's market area. If the business is located in California and all of the customers are in California, then it is unreasonable for the covenant not to compete to preclude the seller from opening a similar business in Florida or New York or anywhere other than California. The third item is compensation. The amount and timing of payments to the seller should be specified. The fourth item is damages. If the seller violates the agreement, what will the amount of the damages be? It is best to settle upon a specific amount. Usually the amount decreases over time: if the breach occurs in the first year, damages will be a certain amount; if it occurs in the second year, it is a lesser amount.

Covenants are desirable to the buyer for several reasons. First, the buyer is assured that the seller will not destroy the business by opening up shop down the street to compete against the buyer. The second advantage is that the portion of the purchase price related to the covenant can be deferred. Payment is made evenly throughout the length of the covenant. The third advantage is that even though the payments are deferred there is no interest expense associated with the payments. The fourth advantage is that payments related to the covenant are tax deductible as a normal and reasonable business expense.

The seller accepts a covenant not to compete for two reasons. The first is that the buyer's request that the seller not compete with the business is reasonable. It is unethical for a seller to sell a business and then to compete with that business. The second reason is financial. A seller can often get a higher price for a business if a portion of the purchase price is related to a covenant not to compete.

Employment Contracts

An employment contract is a contract offered to the seller to become an employee of the buyer after the sale is finalized. Often the buyer wants the seller's experience and expertise. The buyer feels more comfortable knowing an experienced, qualified professional is running the business. With this assurance the buyer may be willing to pay more for the business.

One of the risks of an employment contract is that the seller may find it impossible to be an employee. Frequently a business owner who has had the freedom to make important decisions without critique and review by a superior finds it very difficult to accept supervision.

An employee contract should be specific. In addition to addressing the length of employment and compensation, it should spell out what authority the seller will have as an employee; what the scope, responsibilities, and goals of the job will be. It should provide guidelines as to when the seller can make a decision and when approval must be sought.

The contract should also provide guidelines in case either party finds the employment relationship to be unworkable. What are the financial and other obligations of both parties? It is advisable to make the employment agreement separate from the selling documents, so that if the employment agreement doesn't work out it will not unravel the sale.

A Consulting Contract

This is a contract offered to the seller by the buyer. In exchange for the seller's services the buyer will guarantee to pay the seller a specified amount for a defined period of time.

The advantages of a consulting contract to the buyer are 1) the seller is available to help if something goes wrong or if the job of managing the business is more difficult than expected; 2) a portion of the payment for the business is deferred from the close of the transaction until the consulting contract calls for payment; 3) there is no interest on the payment; and 4) the consulting payments are tax deductible.

The advantages of a consulting contract to a seller are 1) continued involvement in the business; 2) involvement in the continued success of the business; and 3) a higher purchase price for the business.

A seller often finds it difficult to let go of the business. A consulting contract allows the seller to remain involved. As a respected consultant, the former owner can provide input for the ongoing success and growth of the company. This is very important when there are notes payable or other future payments to the seller. If the business fails, these future payments are in jeopardy.

Consulting contracts are usually worded so that the seller receives a specified amount of money on a monthly, quarterly, or annual basis. In return, the seller will make himself or herself available for a specified number of hours or days each month. While the contract requires the seller to be available, the use of the former owner's services is at the discretion of the buyer. Therefore, the consulting agreement should be such that the payments to the seller are made even if the buyer does not use the offered consulting services. The agreement should also provide for additional compensation if the specified amount of consulting time is exceeded.

The seller also needs to be careful that the consulting compensation is reasonable. Excessive compensation may result in an IRS

audit. Also the consulting agreement, like an employment contract, should be separate from the sales documents. The failure of
the consulting arrangement should not result in the sale being ne-
gated.

SELLER'S RISK

Different deal structures present varying degrees of risk to the
seller. Most sellers intuitively understand the risks involved. Basically, the risks include the payment of the purchase price, the timing of the payments and interest payments. In other words, the
seller's worries include:

"I won't get paid."

"I will get paid but the payments will be late."

"I will get paid the principal but not the interest."

"I won't get paid a fair interest rate."

There is one other important risk to consider. That risk is: "I
won't get paid as much for my business as I should." Negotiating
the structure of a deal is an art. By effectively using the different
deal structure methods, the seller encourages the buyer to pay
more for the business. When the buyer sees that the payments are
spread out over time and some of the risk is reduced, he or she is
willing to pay a higher price. The art of deal structuring is in balancing the risks of nonpayment with the risk of selling the business for less than it is worth.

Sometimes a buyer can be found who will pay a fair price for
a business and will pay all cash. Unfortunately, such buyers are
rare—most do not have the financial resources or the desire to pay
entirely in cash. These buyers will demand that the deal be structured to meet their objectives.

BUYER'S RISK

The buyer faces significant risks when purchasing a business. If
the seller helps to reduce or remove some of these risks through

effective deal structuring, then the buyer may reward the seller with a higher price for the business.

Like the seller, the buyer has fears and worries. The buyer's worries include:

"Where can I get the cash to buy this business?"

"Will the business continue to do well after I take over?"

"After I buy it will it provide a good return?"

"Will the profits be enough to make the payments?"

"After the debt payments will there be anything left over for my salary?"

Most of these concerns can be dispelled through effective deal structuring. Providing for fair, adequately secured future payments alleviates the first worry. Having a good employment or consulting contract and an adequate covenant not to compete alleviates concerns about the business continuing to do well. Remember, the primary purpose of deal structuring is to balance the seller's needs with the buyers needs to put together a deal that is advantageous to both parties.

BALANCING THE RISK

The seller seeks adequate security and a good price for his or her business. The buyer seeks an affordable business and a reasonable investment. While good deal structuring can meet both objectives, it cannot make an overpriced business affordable nor can it enable an undercapitalized buyer to purchase a business.

The table which follows lists the seven basic deal structuring techniques and their relevant risks.

The table identifies who accepts the risk of different types of deal structuring techniques. With cash it is obvious that 100 percent of the risk lies with the buyer and none with the seller. However, the other techniques are not so definitive. In most cases some of the risk lies with both parties. The table identifies the party who assumes the greater risk.

Technique	Buyer's Risk	Seller's Risk
Cash	Great	Small
Seller Notes		
Secured	Great	Small
Unsecured	Small	Great
Stock	Small	Varies
Earn Out	Small	Great
Covenant Not		
to Compete	Small	Great
Employment		
Contract	Small	Great
Consulting		
Contract	Small	Great

In the case of a stock purchase, the risk to the seller depends on the nature of the stock and the restrictive agreements. If the stock is publicly traded, there are no restrictive covenants and the block of stock is not large enough to effect the market price, then there is only a small amount of risk to the seller. However, if there are restrictive agreements or if the stock is not publicly traded, there could be substantial risks to the seller.

The question which must be answered is, "What amount of risk is fair for the seller to assume?" No one can answer that question but the seller. The seller's individual needs and desires for security will greatly influence the answer. Also the seller's belief in the business's ability to grow and prosper will influence his or her willingness to accept future payments which depend on the buyer's ability to operate the business.

If the seller needs a lot of cash out of the business to start a new business or to put into some other investment, then the deal structure will have to include a large cash down payment. If the seller is retiring and is concerned about future income, then a large note payable or consulting contract may be in order. If the probable buyer is an owner/operator, the deal should be structured to allow the buyer to pay a reasonable amount down and pay for the remainder in the future.

HOW VALUATION METHODOLOGY AFFECTS DEAL STRUCTURE

In Chapter 8, "Value: Determining the Company's Worth," three primary methods of valuation were discussed. They included synergistic valuation, earnings valuation, and asset valuation. Relying heavily on any one of these valuation methodologies could affect the deal structure.

Synergistic Valuation

The buyer using the synergistic approach to value is purchasing the company to gain access to some unique quality which will geometrically increase the value of the buyer's existing company.

Usually the acquiring company is much larger and has substantial resources relative to the acquired company. Also the purchase price is small relative to the expected benefit. Because of these two factors the purchase price should be primarily a cash transaction. The potential benefit to the acquiring company is such that they are willing to accept all of the risk.

The exception to an all-cash transaction is the case of a questionable or untested synergistic quality. In circumstances where an implementation period is required to determine the success of the synergism, the acquiring company will want the deal structure to include contingent payments based on the success experienced during the implementation period.

Earnings Valuation

The buyer using the earnings approach to value is purchasing an expected stream of future earnings. The risk to the buyer is the risk associated with achieving the earnings. Because the buyer's reward (future earnings) will not be received for some time, the buyer desires to correlate as much as possible the payment for the business with the receipt of future earnings.

The buyer will probably propose a deal structure which includes a down payment of cash along with future payments in the form of a note payable, covenant not to compete, consulting contract, or some other form of payment. Because the buyer is valuing the company based on earnings, he or she desires to pay for as much of the business as possible out of earnings.

Asset Valuation

The buyer using an asset valuation is purchasing the company based on the actual value of its assets. The risk to the buyer is substantially less because he or she is purchasing a tangible asset that has an identifiable market value. Because of this, the seller should expect to receive an offer that is primarily cash. If a note payable is included in the offer, it should be adequately secured and collateralized.

The much-discussed leveraged buy outs (LBO) are purchases using the asset valuation method. In an LBO situation the buyer borrows from a lender using the assets of the company as security. The money received from the loans is used to pay the seller. The buyer then pays off the loan from future company operations. An LBO can be an excellent way to sell a company. Because the buyer is borrowing nearly all of the purchase price from a third party, the seller receives all or nearly all of the purchase price in cash.

THE LEVERAGE OF COMPANY ASSETS

The value of the company's assets and their suitability to be used as collateral affects deal structure. A company with substantial assets and a strong balance sheet should be able to receive a substantial cash down payment.

Acquisition professionals sometimes say that the earnings determine the value and the assets (balance sheet) determine the terms. The stronger the balance sheet, the larger the percentage of the purchase price the seller will receive as a cash down payment. The weaker the balance sheet, the larger the percentage of the purchase price that will be in future payments.

WHAT ABOUT TAXES?

The tax situation of the buyer and the taxable nature of the purchase price will affect the amount the buyer will be willing to offer for the purchase of the business.

If the payments made to the seller are tax deductible for the buyer, then they are in effect partially subsidized by the government. This means the buyer can afford to pay more for the business than if the payments were not tax deductible.

The more a seller can structure the deal towards tax deductible payments, the higher the price that can be demanded. There is a tradeoff however—the types of payments which are tax deductible for the buyer are the methods of payment which are more risky for the seller.

Let's look at each of the seven methods of payment described earlier and examine whether they are tax deductible for the buyer.

Cash—Cash is deductible only if the purchase is a purchase of assets and the assets are depreciable. If it is a stock sale, the cash payment for the stock is not tax deductible.

Notes—The same rule that applies for cash applies for the principle payments of a note. They are deductible only if assets are purchased and the assets are depreciable. However, payments made by the buyer for interest expense are tax deductible.

Stock—Stock or any other payment in kind is considered the same as cash for tax purposes. Stock is desirable to the buyer because it is usually much cheaper for the buyer to dilute the equity of the company than to pay cash.

Earn Out—An earn out may or may not be tax deductible to the buyer depending on how the transaction is structured.

Covenant Not to Compete—A covenant not to compete is normally a tax deductible expense to the buyer, similar to normal salary and wage expenses.

Employment Contract—An employment contract is a tax deductible expense because it is considered a normal salary expense of the company.

Consulting Contract—A consulting contract is a tax deductible expense to the buyer as it is considered a normal operating expense of the company.

Just because an item is tax deductible to the buyer does not mean that the price can be inflated unnecessarily. The best a seller can expect is for the buyer to increase the price for the amount of the offset taxes.

The amount by which a buyer will actually increase an offer is a matter of negotiation. While a buyer will usually offer a higher price if the payments are tax deductible, the amount of the increase will vary depending on the situation and objectives of the buyer.

The point to be made here is that the seller is most likely to get the highest price for the business if he or she cooperates with the buyer and structures as much of the purchase price as is reasonable as tax deductible payments for the buyer.

Much has been said about the tax benefits for the buyer. What about the seller's taxes? In today's tax environment, the form of payment does not affect the seller's tax liability. The seller is usually indifferent to the form of payment regarding taxes because the capital gains tax rate is currently identical to the ordinary income tax rate—the maximum rate for both being 28 percent.

If the capital gains or ordinary income tax rates change, the seller will probably prefer to receive payment in the form that has the lowest tax rate.

SUMMARY AND CONCLUSIONS

Structuring a sales transaction involves determining the amount, timing, and form of payments which the seller will receive for the purchase of the business. It also includes determining the interest rates on future payments as well as the appropriate security or collateral.

When structuring a sale, the seller is faced with a tradeoff. Deal structuring involves balancing the two major risks to the seller—the risk of not getting paid with the risk of selling the business for less than it is worth.

If the seller demands a deal structure which is all cash at the close, the risk of not getting paid is eliminated but the risk of selling the business for less than it is worth increases. If the seller accepts a deal structure with no down payment, or only a small down payment, and substantial future payments, then just the opposite occurs.

The art of deal structuring involves 1) understanding the seller and the seller's needs; 2) understanding the buyer and the buyer's objectives; 3) understanding the business and its resources; and 4) balancing all three with the appropriate deal structuring techniques. It is not an easy task. However, if done properly, the seller will receive the highest value for the business and the buyer will gain ownership of a business which will meet his or her objectives and earn a good return on investment.

Chapter 17
Creative Financing

WHAT IS CREATIVE FINANCING?

In the area of mergers and acquisitions, creative financing is any unique or new form of financing used to finance the purchase. Because it is creative, new, and changing it cannot specifically be defined as this method or that method. The simplest way to describe creative financing is to define what it is not. In Chapter 16, "Structuring the Sale," seven methods of financing were discussed. They included cash, notes payable, stock, an earn out, a covenant not to compete, an employment contract, and a consulting contract. Creative financing is anything not included in these commonly used methods of financing.

The methods of creative financing are limited only by the ingenuity of the buyer, the seller, and their advisors. New methods of creative financing are constantly being developed. Some methods of creative financing are truly ingenious and will be adapted and used in many transactions. Other methods will not provide the desired advantages, and eventually will be discarded.

THE PURPOSE OF CREATIVE FINANCING

If you were to ask a buyer or seller to explain why a method of creative financing was used in a transaction, the most likely answer would be that it was the only way by which they could successfully complete the transaction. This is only a partial truth. Creative financing is often the only way that allows a buyer to get the terms desired and the seller to get the price desired.

Creative financing, in order to be successful, must accomplish two things. First, it must allow the buyer to buy the business with little or no down payment, with the remaining payments spread out over as long a period as possible. Second, it must provide the seller a higher price than could be obtained through more traditional means of financing. Every successful method of creative financing must have both of these characteristics. If it does not, then it has a basic flaw and, while it may be used, it probably will not last.

Many methods which are devised possess only one of the two characteristics. They are supported by a buyer desiring to take advantage of a seller or a seller desiring to take advantage of a buyer. These methods and the people who practice them give the phrase "creative financing" a negative connotation.

Another common characteristic of creative financing methods is that all or a great portion of the purchase price will be paid out of the future profits of the business. Creative financing methods will not work unless the industry and economy will allow the business to grow. Nor will they work unless the buyer has the experience, skill, and resources to make the business grow.

The final significant characteristic of all creative financing methods is risk. The risks to both the buyer and the seller are increased. For the seller, all other things being equal, if the term of payment is extended, then the risk has increased. For the buyer, if the amount of future loan payments go up, then the risk of being unable to meet those payments increases as well.

THE RISKS OF CREATIVE FINANCING

The risks of creative financing are the same as the risks of more traditional financing methods, with the important difference that with creative financing methods those risks loom even larger.

For the seller there are basically four risks: 1) the loss of principal payments; 2) the loss of interest payments; 3) the delay in receiving principal or interest payments; and 4) the possibility of having to take back the company.

For the buyer there is one basic risk—what will happen if business operations do not provide enough cash to make the payments?

An interesting fact of creative financing is that both the buyer's and seller's risks are directly related to the future success of the business. If the business grows and increases in profitability and value, then there will be no problem. If the business does not grow, then everyone has problems.

ANALYZING CREATIVE FINANCING PROPOSALS

Creative financing methods are analyzed the same way as all other financing methods. There are basically three steps. The first step is to identify the amount and timing of all the payments that are to be received. The second step is to assess the risk of each payment and determine an appropriate risk factor (rate of return). The third and final step is to determine, based on the payment amount and the risk factor, the net present value of all the payments. In Chapter 18, "The Offer," a detailed discussion about analyzing offers is presented.

Many business owners will not consider creative financing methods at all. This attitude is an extreme, but it reminds us that caution is required. Creative financing may enable a seller to increase the price received for the business, but there is additional risk associated with the higher price. The most frequent and most significant mistake seller's make when analyzing creative financing is underestimating that risk.

The success of creative financing almost always hinges on the assumption that the business will grow or somehow be significantly more profitable in the future. Because of this unique characteristic, extra care and effort need to be taken in several areas of the analysis, including buyer expertise, buyer resources, seller involvement, market analysis, pro forma financial analysis, and sensitivity analysis.

Buyer Expertise

It is the buyer's task to increase the sales and profits of the company. If this is not done, there will not be enough funds to pay off the seller.

An investigation must be performed by the seller to assure that the buyer possesses all of the expertise and skills that will be required. If the buyer is found deficient, then the transaction and the future success of the business are doomed to failure.

Undoubtedly the buyer will have a plan for the future success of the company. Review the plan and discuss it with the buyer. Make sure the plan is reasonable, and that the timing is not overly aggressive. Check the plan to see that there are contingency plans in case of failure. The purpose of this review is not to destroy the plan, but rather to strengthen the plan to make it as foolproof as possible.

Buyer Resources

Once it is determined that the buyer has the expertise, then it must be determined that the buyer has the resources. Resources are anything that will be needed to accomplish the buyer's plans for growth. They may include a management team, the expansion of facilities, working capital, or other items. Many capable business managers with excellent business plans have failed because they were unable to obtain the required resources to carry out their plans.

Seller Involvement

No one knows the company better than the seller. The seller should also be an expert on the industry, marketplace, and competitors. With this knowledge and experience the seller can become a valued advisor to the buyer. The seller's involvement is also important because the future payments to the seller are directly related to the future success of the business. Thus, agreements which permit the seller some involvement in the future operations of the company are common. The seller will often serve as a director or consultant, sharing his or her expertise and experience when necessary.

Involving the seller also has another advantage: a seller who is involved and knows the facts of the situation is less likely to make the buyer/seller relationship adversarial. If the business fails to perform as expected the seller understands why. This makes it easier to approach the problems of the business and resolve how the seller will receive payment for the company.

Market Analysis

The success achieved through growth and increased profitability is dependent on external as well as internal factors. The external factors include the general economic condition of the region, the country, the market or markets which the company serves, and the industry in which the company participates. The specific characteristics of these external factors will affect the buyer's ability to achieve growth.

The growth, or lack of growth, in the marketplace and industry affect the success of the company. It is very difficult for a company to grow rapidly if the market is only growing at an annual rate of 2 percent. Increasing profits will be difficult if the industry has excess capacity and competitors begin to cut prices.

Market analysis consists of researching the industry and marketplace to assure that the assumptions in the buyer's plan for growth are reasonable. If they are not reasonable, the plan needs to be revised. A thorough market analysis often suggests ways in which a company can grow or increase its profitability.

Pro Forma Financial Analysis

The pro forma financial analysis is the projection of what the future financial statements of the company will look like after the implementation of the buyer's plan. Statements commonly included are income statements, balance sheets (or portions thereof), and cash flow statements.

Pro forma financial statements, while based on the buyer's plan for growth, should be supported by the operating history of the company and the market analysis which was performed. The seller should require pro forma statements for as far into the future as the debt structure of the sale requires.

These are the statements which support the claim that the buyer will be able to pay off the purchase debt to the seller. They must be based on reasonable assumptions.

Sensitivity Analysis

Remember that buyers and business people are rarely 100 percent on target. Sensitivity analysis is a method devised to determine what would happen if the buyer achieved something less than 100 percent of the business plan.

In other words, sensitivity analysis is analyzing what would happen if there were variations in the basic assumptions. For example, if the sales forecast assumed that the industry would grow at 8 percent per year and the company would grow at 16 percent per year, what would happen if the industry grew only 3 percent per year? How would this affect the pro forma financial analysis? Another example: how would future profitability be affected if a facility expansion that was supposed to cost $150,000 actually cost $250,000? In every plan there are usually several alternatives to consider.

In sensitivity analysis one identifies the critical assumptions of the analysis and repeats the analysis assuming a lower level of success. This will focus attention on those areas which are most critical for success. It will also help you shape a picture of what will happen if the buyer is only partially successful.

CREATIVE FINANCING METHODS

There is no limit on the number and type of creative financing methods. As long as sellers look for ways to increase the purchase price and as long as buyers look for ways to lower the down payment, new methods will be developed. The following is a discussion of a few creative financing methods. These methods were selected for one of two reasons: either they are, in the opinion of the author, very creative, or they are methods which are fairly common.

The Supportable Debt Method

This method allows the seller to sell the business for a lot of money and allows the buyer to buy the company with no cash outlay. Unfortunately, this method will work for only a limited number of sellers and buyers. Also, it often takes several years to complete the total sale of the business.

For the supportable debt method to work, the company being sold must be a rapidly growing, highly profitable firm. This method works well with service type companies which, relative to their profitability, have only a small investment in assets. The buyer must be a firm with significant borrowing capabilities. This method works very nicely when the buyer is a large corporation with significant borrowing ability.

The method is somewhat complicated and can best be explained with an example. The selling company is a rapidly growing service firm which provides technical consulting services to other corporations. The firm has been in existence for about ten years. Operating profit for the year that is just ending will be $2.5 million. Profits have grown in excess of 25 percent per year for the last several years and management expects growth of 20 percent or more for at least the next three to five years.

The owner of the company wants to cash out. The owner recognizes that the company's value is substantial and wants to use part of that value for other things. The owner feels the future is promising and would like to be involved for at least a few years as part of that future success.

The seller decides to try to sell the company using the supportable debt method. With this method the amount of debt which the company could support with its current earnings is determined. The assumptions include a borrowing rate at or near the prime rate and a payback period of three to five years. In this instance, assuming a prime rate of 10 percent, a five-year payback, and pretax profit of $2.5 million, the company can support debt of about $9.5 million.

In addition to the supportable debt amount, a good forecast of future earnings is required. If we assume, as projected by the management of the company, that profits will increase 20 percent per year, then in three years the pretax profits of the company will be $4.3 million. In five years they will be $6.2 million.

Having gathered this information, the company now approaches potential buyers with a proposition. The buyer will use his or her borrowing power to borrow $9.5 million. This money will be used to purchase 49 percent of the company from the current owner. The payoff of the debt will be made by the seller's company over the five-year life of the loan.

After five years the debt will be paid off and the buying company will have a 49 percent interest in a company with annual profits of $6.2 million. This equity interest will have been obtained with no cash outlay; the only requirements having been obtaining and guaranteeing the loan.

After the initial transaction, there are many additional options. Because the seller eventually wants out of the company, there is usually an additional agreement between the buyer and the seller. Such an agreement could give the buying company the right to buy out the 51 percent interest after two or three or four years. It could call for the sale of the company after a few years with the seller taking 51 percent of the proceeds and the buying company (now one of the sellers) taking 49 percent. Or it may call for taking the company public at some point in the future.

This method of financing is indeed creative. The seller receives $9.5 million for 49 percent of a company with profits of $2.5 million. The buyer receives the 49 percent interest without having to make any cash outlay. If the business is resold after three or four years, the seller will receive additional monies—51 percent of the selling price.

This method meets all the criteria of creative financing. The seller receives substantially more for the business. To some it would seem as if the seller sells the business twice and is paid twice. The buyer obtains a significant interest in the business with no cash outlay. The risk of the transaction is the risk of all creative financing methods if the profitability of the business does not increase as planned or perhaps even declines, what happens to the outstanding loan? The future plans of both parties are jeopardized.

The Leveraged Buy Out Method

The leveraged buy out (LBO) is a common method of financing a business. Some people may challenge whether this is in fact a creative financing method. The fact is, the LBO is a creative financing method that has been so successful that it has become commonplace.

The typical selling company in an LBO is an asset intensive company with low profits relative to the value of the assets. The company is in a situation where the level of profits does not support or justify the value or borrowing capability of the assets. The buyer, using the assets as collateral, borrows all or nearly all of the purchase price. The seller is paid a price which is substantially higher than the earnings would justify and the buyer, because of the borrowing power of the assets, buys the company with little or no down payment.

Let's look at a specific example. The LBO Company has been in business for fifty years. The company is conservatively managed and has always been profitable. Last year's profits before tax were approximately a million dollars. Next year's profits will be about a million dollars, maybe slightly more. The company has two unique product lines. Profits for product line A are about $300,000. Profits for product line B are about $700,000.

The company is an asset-intensive manufacturing concern. Over the years it has acquired a lot of manufacturing equipment that is still very valuable and useful. In fact, much of it is worth as much today as when it was bought—or more. The company also owns its facilities. Today they are worth much more than when they were purchased. Recent appraisals show that the fair market value of the company's assets is $7,000,000. The company is debt-free.

The owner/general manager of the firm has decided to retire. He is the son of the founder. His children have expressed no desire to take over the business, so the decision is made to sell. The owner determines that given the risks and opportunities of the company and the industry, the business is worth about $3.5 to $4.0 million. This value is based on the earnings of the company.

A group of individuals decide that they are interested in the firm and want to attempt an LBO. After consulting a number of lenders, they find that they can borrow $5 million using the assets of the company as collateral. With this knowledge they make an offer of $4.5 million cash on the business.

The owner of LBO Company is delighted. The offer is accepted. The LBO group borrows $4.5 million using the assets of the company as collateral, pays the owner, and takes possession of the business.

The business in its current state cannot support a $4.5 million debt. Changes must be made—the buyers know this, and they have a plan. Their analysis shows that product line A, which produces $300,000 a year in profits, had about $3,000,000 of assets supporting it; and Product line B, which produces $700,000 a year in profits, has about $4,000,000 of assets supporting it.

The plan is to liquidate product line A. This is done. The buyers receive $3,000,000 in cash from the liquidation, which they use to pay off $2,500,000 of the bank debt. The remaining $500,000 is invested in updating the production facilities of product line B. The debt of the company has now been reduced from $4,500,000 to $2,000,000.

The new management team is more aggressive than the previous owner. Because of this, and as a result of the $500,000 investment, the buyers are able to increase the profitability of product line B from $700,000 a year to $850,000 a year. The buyers now own a company that earns $850,000 a year and has $2,000,000 in debt, a comfortable amount that can be paid off in three to five years.

The preceeding example is simple, yet it illustrates how an LBO works. An asset-intensive, low-profit company is purchased. The assets of the company are used to collateralize the purchase price, which is borrowed from a third party or perhaps from the owner. Once the buyers gain control, they reorganize the business to make it less asset-intensive and more efficient. Often, a portion of the business is liquidated or sold off to provide the cash needed to reduce the debt to acceptable levels.

The end results of this creative financing technique are (1) a seller receives a high price compared to the earnings value of the company; (2) a buyer purchases the company for little or no down payment; and (3) a company is reorganized, usually in a more efficient manner than before.

A question often posed is, "If the buyer could reorganize the business and make it more valuable, why couldn't the seller?" The truth is, in most cases, the seller could. However, for various reasons, the seller does not. Perhaps the seller does not see the opportunity. Perhaps in our example, product line A was the original product line of the company and the seller could not, for emotional or sentimental reasons, liquidate it. Sellers often see opportunities but just don't have the desire to put forth the effort and take the risks necessary to take advantage of them.

The Leaseback of Assets Method

Frequently a company being sold may have substantial assets relative to the selling price. However, unlike the LBO scenario, these assets do not have significant borrowing power. The assets may be a fleet of vehicles or perhaps some customized machinery. The assets are critical to the ongoing operations of the firm, but the bank won't lend a significant amount of money against them.

When such situations occur, buyers frequently do not have the cash required to purchase the company. The solution is to sell the business *without* these assets. The seller retains ownership of the assets and leases them to the buyer. The lease provides for payments to the seller for a specified period of time. At the expiration of the lease, the buyer has the option to purchase the assets for a nominal amount.

The advantage of this method is that it allows the buyer to purchase the business when otherwise he or she would not have the financial means to do so. It also allows the seller to get a higher price for the business than would otherwise be possible. The seller's risk is also protected somewhat as the seller retains title to the assets which are subject to the lease.

Chapter 18

The Offer

WHAT IS AN OFFER?

An offer to purchase a business is a proposal from a prospective buyer indicating his or her desire to purchase the company, and presenting the proposed price, terms, and conditions of the purchase. The offer is often called a "letter of intent" because it is often in letter form and it sets forth the intent of the buyer to buy the business and the seller to sell it. Once the terms and conditions have been agreed upon, the letter of intent is signed by both parties.

As well as setting forth the price, terms, and conditions of the purchase, the letter of intent precludes the seller from negotiating with or offering the business to other buyers. The letter of intent will also give the buyer the authority to perform due diligence. Due diligence is the term used to describe the formal analysis and investigation of the company which the buyer needs to complete before the transaction is finalized.

The offer also includes a deposit towards the purchase price, which is often non-refundable. The deposit demonstrates the buyer's good faith and protects the seller against the time and effort lost if the sale does not go through.

WHAT AN OFFER IS NOT

An offer is not a final binding purchase contract. The letter of intent only sets forth the buyers intent to purchase, *providing certain events occur*. These events include such factors as the buyer obtaining financing; the business receiving a clean opinion from the due diligence; and the attorneys being able to draft formal acquisition documents which are acceptable to both parties.

The letter of intent is usually written in a way that allows the buyer to cancel the purchase if he or she so desires. Sellers needn't be overly concerned about the buyer's escape clauses—the buyer is simply taking precautionary measures. The buyer wants to buy the company—otherwise, no offer would have been made. But the buyer seeks protection in case the more detailed examination of the company uncovers something detrimental to the expected future of the company.

The seller's attorney should review the letter of intent carefully, and make sure that all escape clauses are identified and understood by the seller. If they are reasonable, accept them. If they are not reasonable, ask that they be deleted from the offer.

In actual practice only about half of the offers extended and accepted result in a finalized transaction. The failure to close the transaction can be the result of the actions of either party. The seller decides to call off the deal just about as often as the buyer.

HOW TO GET THE DEAL STRUCTURE YOU WANT

To obtain an offer with a deal structure that meets the seller's needs, the seller must follow these steps:

1. Identify upfront the structure that fits the seller's needs. What would be most desirable to the seller?

2. Make sure that the seller's needs are compatible with the characteristics of the business.

3. In the negotiation sessions with interested buyers, explain what the seller's needs are and why.

Buyers realize that the more they meet the seller's needs, the better their chances of success. Therefore, they will structure the offer to meet the seller's needs if at all possible.

One of the first steps in selling a business is identifying the seller's goals and objectives. If the seller is realistic in identifying what he or she wants to accomplish by selling the business, then these needs can be met with the appropriate deal structure.

A frequent problem involves adapting the deal structure to the nature of business. For instance, a seller may want an all-cash deal, but the nature of the business is such that a buyer is reluctant to pay all cash. The deal structure must balance the seller's needs and the buyer's objectives with the realities of the business. Compromise and the ability to accept the facts of the situation are an important part of accomplishing this.

During the negotiation sessions the buyer is trying to accomplish two things. First, the buyer needs to get enough information about the business to make the purchase decision. Second, the buyer tries to determine what the seller wants and needs from the sale of the business. By directly telling the buyer what the seller's needs are, the negotiations are made easier all around. The chance of success is also increased, as the buyer will know how to structure an offer that the seller will accept. Also, if the buyer knows the seller will accept a flexible deal structure, he or she may be encouraged. The buyer knows that he or she is dealing with someone who understands the needs of both parties and is willing to cooperate to see that everyone is satisfied.

WHEN WILL AN OFFER BE MADE?

As explained in Chapter 15, "Negotiating," the best method to use when selling a company is the auction method. This method provides a timetable which specifies a period when offers will be accepted. If the auction method is not being used, you must deal with buyers as you find them and offers when you get them.

Usually the buyer will go through a three-step process before making an offer: 1) learn about the company and review the important documents; 2) examine the physical facilities; and 3) analyze and negotiate to determine the value of the company to the buyer and the seller's wants and needs. A buyer almost never makes an offer until these three tasks have been completed.

EXAMPLES OF OFFERS

The business has been on the market for some time. Several buyers have shown an interest. They have visited the facility and studied the detailed business analysis. Several conversations and negotiating sessions have been held with each interested buyer. It has been requested that all interested parties have their offers to purchase submitted by the end of the month. The seller is anxiously waiting to see how many offers will be received and what the offering prices will be.

The offers received could include any combination of deal structure methods. The total price could vary over a wide range. Let's look at seven different offers which could be received for the same business. The offering prices range from $1,600,000 to $2,500,000. As you read each of the offers, think about the business's and the seller's needs. Which of the components of the different offers would or would not be acceptable and why?

The seven offers are as follows:

1. This is an all-cash offer. $ 1,600,000

   $1,600,000 will be paid to the seller at the close of the transaction.

2. This is an all-stock offer. $ 1,890,000

   The purchaser is a public company. The seller will receive 42,000 shares of the stock of the company with a market value of $45 per share, or $1,890,000. The sale of the stock, however, is restricted. No stock can be sold for thirty days. No more than 5,000 shares can be sold in any thirty-day period and no more than 14,000 shares can be sold in any twelve-month period.

3. This offer includes a cash down
   payment and a secured note. $ 1,700,000

A down payment of $400,000 will be paid at the close of the transaction. A note payable in the amount of $1,300,000 will be executed. The note will be a five-year note with annual principal and interest payments. The interest rate of the note is 10 percent. The note is fully secured by the assets of the business and by sufficient personal assets of the buyer.

4. This offer includes a cash down
   payment and stock. $ 2,000,000

The seller will receive $500,000 at the close plus 500,000 shares of stock in the acquiring company. The acquiring company is privately held. There is no public market for the stock. The seller is informed, however, that the value of the stock is estimated to be $3 per share, resulting in a total stock value of $1,500,000.

The seller has also been asked to remain with the acquiring company as a vice president and member of the board of directors. The salary to be received by the seller is a fair market salary. The 500,000 shares of stock give the seller a 20 percent interest in the company. There are four other stockholders, one with a 45 percent interest, one with a 20 percent interest, and two 7.5 percent interests.

If things go well, the company will be taken public in three to five years. If revenue and profit projections are met, the value of the stock, when taken public, should be between $7 and $8 a share.

5. This offer includes a cash down
   payment, a secured note, and an
   employment contract. $ 2,100,000

A cash down payment of $500,000 will be paid at the close. The note payable will be for $1,000,000 and will be fully secured, payable in annual principal, and interest payments over five years with a 10 percent interest rate.

The employment contract is for three years. The seller will be president of the company and will report to the buyer, who will be the chairman of the board. The president's annual salary will be $200,000 per year. A fair salary for the position is $100,000 per year.

6. This offer includes a cash down payment
   and a note that will be secured only
   by the assets of the business. $ 1,850,000

The down payment paid at the close will be $400,000. The note will be a $1,450,000 note payable in annual principal and interest payments over seven years. The interest rate will be 10 percent.

In addition, the buyer informs you that he or she will be borrowing $250,000 from the bank to be used as part of the down payment. The $1,450,000 note will be subordinated to the bank debt.

7. This offer includes a cash down
   payment, a secured note, an
   employment contract, and an earn out. $ 2,500,000

The down payment at the close will be $400,000. The secured note will be a $900,000 note payable over five years with annual principal and interest payments. The interest rate of the note will be 10 percent. The employment contract will be for four years and the salary paid will be $100,000 per year.

The earn out is a contingent payment based on growth in revenue and pretax profits. The seller will receive a bonus based on the increase in revenue and a percentage of the increase in pretax profits. If the company grows at an average rate of 25 percent per year, the total earn out payments received will be $800,000. A payment will be made at the end of each year. It is anticipated that the payments will be $50,000 at the end of the first year, $150,000 at the end of the second, $250,000 at the end of the third, and $350,000 at the end of the fourth. If revenue and profit grow at less than 25 percent, the contingent payment will be decreased accordingly. If the company grows at a rate of less than 10 percent, the seller will receive no earn out payments.

These seven offers include examples of all of the common forms of payment. The purchase price ranges from a low of $1,600,000 to a high of $2,500,000, yet in terms of economic value they are all about the same. The difference comes from the difference in the timing of the payments and the risks associated with the different forms of payments.

As a seller examines different offers and deal structures, such as those presented above, he or she will be able to identify what is and is not an acceptable offer. Some of the deal structures will be totally unacceptable. Others will be pretty close to what the seller really wants. There are probably others which the seller would consider, but he or she needs to think them through before a decision can be made.

Some of the offers are more desirable financially. Others provide more security. The timing of payments may fit the seller's needs better in one offer than in another. Some options allow the seller to begin to cash out while still remaining very involved in the business. Some allow the seller to partially cash out now while offering the chance of bigger returns down the road.

The key to choosing well depends on the seller's needs. Has the seller clearly and honestly defined his or her needs? Has the seller considered emotional and lifestyle needs as well as monetary needs? If the seller has done these things, then choosing the best offer should be a straightforward task.

The seller must also consider the nonfinancial aspects of the offers. If the continued success and growth of the company is important to the seller, he or she may want to give extra weight to an offer from someone who will keep the firm in its present form or provide means for improved growth. There are many nonmonetary factors to consider—many more than most business owners would like to admit.

From a financial standpoint the way to assess which offer is best is to determine which has the highest net present value. Net present value is defined as the value in today's dollars of all the payments related to the sale of the business. When determining the value in today's dollars, the important factors to consider are the timing of the future payments and the level of risk associated with each payment.

To compare the offers, make a schedule that identifies the timing and amount of all payments. Assign a risk factor (often called the discount rate or required rate of return) to the different payments based on how secure they are. Based on this risk factor, determine the net present value of all the payments of each offer. The offer with the highest net present value provides the most economic value to the seller. Such a schedule for the seven offers described earlier has been prepared and is presented in Exhibit 18–1.

Of the seven offers, number 5, which included a cash down payment, an employment contract, and a secured note payable, provides the highest present value. Offer number 2, which was a payment of stock, had the lowest net present value.

The range of net present values for all the offers varied from a low of $1,593,000 to a high of $1,679,000. This range is much narrower than the purchase price range of $1,600,000 and $2,500,000.

When analyzing offers, one of the most important decisions for a seller is determining the appropriate risk factor. The risk factor can be defined as the fair rate of return taking into consideration all of the risks associated with the payments. When determining the risk factor for a payment, two things should be considered. First, is there a similar debt instrument in the marketplace for which rate of return information is available? Second, what is the rate of return the seller would require if he were to purchase a similar debt instrument for investment purposes?

For example, if one of the debt instruments is a secured note, one can go to the public market and find out what interest rate is being charged for loans secured by real estate, machinery and equipment, or other assets. If there is an unsecured note, one can find out what rate is being charged companies that borrow money with little or no security.

The principle of risk versus return should be understood: the higher the risk associated with the debt, the greater the required rate of return. If the deal structure has more than one form of payment, then more than one risk factor needs to be determined.

There are two additional factors to consider which concern the reasons why buyers like sellers to carry financing. The first reason is that sellers usually require a lower interest rate than a bank or other lender. The second reason is that the seller usually requires less collateral than a bank or other lending institution. Keep these in mind when deciding on a risk factor. Unless bank rates were used when determining the interest rate on notes, the risk factor associated with the notes should probably be higher than the stated interest rate.

Employment contracts are often included as part of the purchase price. However, when analyzing an offer, consider only the compensation that is in excess of the fair market salary for the job. A fair salary paid for the seller's employment services is not part of the purchase price; it is payment for services just like any other employment arrangement. The salary paid in an employment contract enters the analysis only if the compensation is in excess of the fair market rate.

Exhibit 18-1 presents a comparison of all seven offers. The following discussion presents an explanation of how each offer was analyzed and how the net present value was calculated.

For purposes of this analysis the following risk factors were used:

Secured Note	12%
Unsecured Note	15%
Employment Contract	15%
Public Stock	20%
Earn Out	30%
Private Stock	35%

These rates are based on historic rates in the marketplace and the author's experience. The rates which you decide to use may vary from these rates.

Offer 1: This is the easiest offer to analyze. $1,600,000 will be received at the close. The total amount received and the net present value is $1,600,000.

Exhibit 18-1 Analysis of Offers

Offer	Purchase Price	Close	Year 1	Year 2	Year 3	Year 4	Year 5	Year 6	Year 7	Total Cash Received	Net Present Value
1. All Cash	$1,600,000	$1,600,000	-0-	-0-	-0-	-0-	-0-	-0-	-0-	$1,600,000	$1,600,000
2. All Stock 42,000 Shares @ $45/Share	$1,890,000	$630,000	$630,000	$630,000	-0-	-0-	-0-	-0-	-0-	$1,890,000	
—Net Present Value		$630,000	$525,000	$438,000							$1,593,000
3. Down Payment Note: $1,300,000 5 yrs, 10%	$1,700,000	$400,000	$343,000	$343,000	$343,000	$343,000	$343,000	-0-	-0-	$2,115,000	
—Net Present Value		$400,000	$306,000	$273,000	$244,000	$218,000	$195,000	-0-	-0-		$1,636,000
4. Down Payment Stock: 500,000 Shares @ $3/Share Sold in 4 yrs @7.50/Share	$2,000,000	$500,000	-0-	-0-	-0-	$3,750,000	-0-	-0-	-0-	$4,250,000	
—Net Present Value		$500,000	-0-	-0-	-0-	$1,129,000	-0-	-0-	-0-		$1,629,000
5. Down Payment Note: $1,000,000 5 yrs, 10 %	$1,800,000	$500,000	$264,000	$264,000	$264,000	$264,000	$264,000	-0-	-0-	$2,120,000	
—Net Present Value			$236,000	$210,000	$188,000	$168,000	$150,000	-0-	-0-		

Employment Contract	$500,000								
–Excess Salary		$100,000	$100,000	$100,000	-0-	-0-	$150,000		
–Net Present Value		$87,000	$76,000	$66,000	$168,000	$254,000	$286,000	$323,000	
Total Present Value									**$1,681,000**
6. Down Payment	$1,850,000								
Notes: $1,450,000									
7 yrs, 10%		$298,000	$298,000	$298,000	$298,000	$298,000	$298,000	$298,000	
–Net Present Value		$259,000	$225,000	$196,000	$170,000	$148,000	$129,000	$112,000	
									$2,486,000
Total Present Value	$400,000								**$1,639,000**
7. Down Payment	$2,100,000								
Notes: $900,000									
5 yrs, 10%	$237,000	$237,000	$237,000	$237,000	$237,000	$237,000			
–Net Present Value	$212,000	$189,000	$169,000	$151,000	$134,000	$134,000			
									$2,385,000
Earn Out	$50,000	$150,000	$250,000	$350,000	-0-	-0-			
–Net Present Value	$38,000	$89,000	$114,000	$123,000	$123,000	$112,000			
Total Present Value	$400,000	$278,000	$283,000	$274,000	$134,000	$134,000			**$1,619,000**

Notes and Assumptions:

1. The discount rates (required rates of return) used were 12% for secured notes, 15% for unsecured notes, 15% for excess salary related to employment contracts, 20% for public stock, 30% for an earn out, and 35% for private stock.

2. When analyzing employment contracts only the compensation in excess of a fair market salary is considered as part of the price of the company.

Offer 2: Payment of 42,000 shares of stock is received. It is assumed that the seller will sell the stock as quickly as the restrictive covenants allow. This means that 14,000 shares will be sold each year for three years. Assuming a price of $45 per share, the payments will be $630,000 per year. Using the risk factor of 20 percent, the net present value of each payment is determined and added together, resulting in a total net present value of $1,593,000.

Offer 3: A down payment of $400,000 is received. As payment on the note, annual payments of $343,000 are received for five years. The net present value of the down payment is $400,000 as it is received at the close of the sale. To determine the net present value of the note payments, a risk factor of 12 percent is used. When totalled, the net present value is $1,636,000.

Offer 4: A down payment of $500,000 is received along with 500,000 shares of stock valued at $3 per share. The stock is not publicly traded but the company plans to go public in three to five years. The expected value when the company goes public is $7 to $8 per share. If we assume that the company goes public in four years with a stock price of $7.50, and the seller cashes out at that time, then the seller will receive $3,750,000 in year 4. When the risk factor of 35 percent is applied to this payment the resulting net present value is $1,129,000. When added to the down payment, the total net present value is $1,629,000.

Offer 5: A down payment of $500,000 is received. Payments relating to the $1,000,000 note of $264,000 per year for five years are received. The employment contract also calls for salary payments in excess of a fair market salary in the amount of $100,000 per year for three years. The risk factor for the secured note is 12 percent. The risk factor for the employment contract is 15 percent. When the net present value from these payments is calculated and added to the down payment, a total net present value of $1,681,000 results.

Offer 6: A down payment of $400,000 is received at the close. Payments related to the note of $298,000 per year are received for seven years. The risk factor for the unsecured note is 15 percent.

When the net present value of the note payments is calculated and added to the down payment, a total net present value of $1,639,000 results.

Offer 7: A down payment of $400,000 is received. Payments of $237,000 per year, related to the secured $900,000 note, are received for five years. Payments from the earn out are received in the amounts of $50,000 in year 1, $150,000 in year 2, $250,000 in year 3 and $350,000 in year 4. The payments from the employment contract are not considered as the salary paid is not in excess of the fair market rate. A risk factor of 12 percent is used to determine the net present value of the note payments and a risk factor of 30 percent is used to determine the net present value of the earn out payments. When these figures are added to the down payment, a total net present value of $1,619,000 results.

The results of the analysis show that there is less than $100,000 difference between the net present value of all of the offers. This was done intentionally to illustrate that what may appear to be wide variations in purchase price are not necessarily wide variations in economic value. A thorough analysis of all the offers must be performed before a wise decision can be made.

SHOPPING AN OFFER

"Shopping an offer" is the practice of going from potential buyer to potential buyer and saying, "I have an offer, here are the price, terms, and conditions—can you beat this deal?"

Few things make a buyer as angry as having an offer shopped around. Many buyers will automatically withdraw an offer if they find out it is being shopped around. Brokers who shop offers soon find that buyers won't work with them. The buyer's offer is made as a result of good faith negotiations and unless other arrangements are made, is assumed to be confidential. There are ways of achieving the best deal without shopping an offer around—it is to the seller's advantage to avoid this practice.

Chapter 19
Due Diligence and Negotiation

Once an offer is accepted and a letter of intent is signed by both parties, the seller will make available to the buyer all of the company's records and documents. The buyer's advisors will analyze this information—the process is called "due diligence." The purpose of the due diligence is twofold. First, the buyer wants to confirm that all of the information about the company which has been received so far is correct. Second, the due diligence team is looking for any previously unidentified facts about the company which may affect the deal. The due diligence team works for the buyer, trying to protect his or her interests. Thus, the nature of the task is adversarial.

The due diligence team consists of experts or advisors selected by the buyer. There are usually four or five advisors. The buyer will have an attorney to analyze the legal position and legal risks of the company. An accountant will review accounting records and procedures. Manufacturing or technical experts will review the technology, processes, and resources of the company's operations. A management expert will review the organization and personnel records of the company. The buyer's banker or financing representative will review those aspects of the company related to the buyer's efforts to obtain financing.

The due diligence analysis is performed at a time and place mutually agreeable to both parties. The time required for the analysis depends on the availability of records, the complexity of the company, and the level of detail desired by the buyer. For some companies the review and analysis can be performed in a day or two; for others the review and analysis can take several months. It is common for the seller to allow the due diligence team on site to collect data, review records, and copy documents. Then the team will have between thirty and ninety days to complete the analysis. Once the analysis is complete, the final acquisition documents will be drafted.

SKELETONS IN THE CLOSET

Psychologically, it is often difficult to reveal detailed and sensitive records of the company to an outsider, especially if that outsider is looking for potential problem areas where perhaps the seller has not done as thorough a job as possible.

The seller may fear that the due diligence team will not only criticize but find serious problems—"skeletons in the closet." The best way for the seller to prepare for the due diligence review is to perform his or her own due diligence review in advance of the buyer's. If the seller has already reviewed those items important to the buyer, then he or she will be able to assist the buyer with confidence.

All company documents and records should be identified and prepared for review. If the necessary documents are up-to-date, complete, and easily available, then the process will proceed smoothly and the outcome will probably be more favorable and more quickly achieved. The sooner the due diligence team can be provided the proper documentation, the sooner the due diligence process will be complete—and the sooner the transaction will be finalized.

Once the seller has found and reviewed the records needed by the buyer, and the seller has performed his or her own due diligence, no unidentified "skeletons" should remain for the buyer to uncover. Also, the buyer probably will be impressed with the organization and efficiency of the organization, which in itself will help lead to a more favorable outcome.

There is no complete list of all the documents needed for due diligence. The buyer may want to examine only a few documents, or may on the other hand want to review all of the documents available in the company's files. The important documents to prepare include any and all significant documents relating to the ongoing operations, liabilities, and commitments of the company. A suggested list is as follows:

- Copies of corporate articles of incorporation and bylaws
- Copies of business licenses, permits, franchise agreements, etc.
- Copies of corporate minutes
- List of all shareholders
- Tax returns for the last three to five years
- Audit letter from the most recently audited financial statements
- Financial statements (all statements for the past three to five years)
- Current and long-term budgets
- Fixed asset schedules and copies of any appraisals
- Bank statements and cancelled checks (three-five years)
- Bank accounts—authorization to sign/borrow
- Copies of loan agreements
- Copies of insurance policies and certificates of insurance
- Copies of all leases
- Copies of all rental agreements
- Complete customer list
- Catalogs, price lists, and other company sales literature
- Accounts receivable aging
- Payroll roster and records
- Copies of any pension or profit-sharing plans including actuarial review of funding adequacy
- Copies of all employment letters or contracts

- Collective bargaining agreements and union contracts
- Organization chart
- Job descriptions
- Details of any litigation, current or over the past few years
- Copies of and details about any patents, copyrights, or proprietary technology.
- Documentation for any proprietary software
- Policy and procedures manuals
- Copies of any sales contracts and agreements
- Copies of any purchase contracts and agreements
- Details of all product warranties
- List of and details about any related companies
- Copies of any other documents relating to any debts, obligations, liabilities, or commitments of the company

NEGOTIATING THE DEAL

It has been several weeks since you completed due diligence—since you spent what seemed like years with the buyer's accountants, attorneys, bankers, and technical people. They asked questions about the smallest details of the business. They wanted copies of almost every document ever produced by the company. Now the phone rings. It is the buyer, who has just finished reviewing the analysis prepared by the due diligence team. Overall, the buyer is pleased with the report; however, there are a few points that need to be discussed. A meeting is arranged.

As the meeting begins the buyer sets the stage by repeating that overall the due diligence review was acceptable, and the buyer's attorneys have been instructed to begin drafting the final acquisition documents. However, some new problems were identified. They are not deal-killing problems, but they do increase the risk of the transaction and must be addressed.

The first risk stems from an accounting practice. The buyer's accountant has discovered that one of the company's tax policies is a practice that is being closely scrutinized by the Internal Revenue

Service. The risk of an audit resulting in an increased tax liability is high. Also, if the procedure is disallowed by the IRS, the company's taxes could be significantly higher in the future. The buyer assures you that this is a small problem, but of concern nevertheless.

There is another risk. The company offers an extended warranty on all of its products. One of the new product lines has started to show a higher than expected repair rate. This may result in a higher warranty service cost which could effect future profits.

The meeting continues. The buyer describes other problems and how they increase the risk of the transaction. When the buyer finishes explaining the newly identified problem areas, the topic switches to financing. The buyer explains that the bank has decided that they can lend only 80 percent of the requested acquisition loan amount. The buyer has investigated other sources of financing, but the responses, unfortunately, have not been encouraging.

The buyer now lays out all the cards. "We still want your company. We feel that it is an attractive company with a good future. But, in the light of these developments, we can't afford to pay the agreed price. However, we can afford to buy the company if the price were discounted ten percent."

It is important to understand the psychology of this negotiation technique. The buyer wants to purchase the company for as low a price as possible. Whenever an opportunity to negotiate a lower price arises, the buyer will try to take advantage of it. The purpose of the due diligence analysis is to confirm the information already received and to identify any possible problems with the deal. In almost every situation some problem is identified. Even if it is small and insignificant, the buyer can use it to attempt to lower the price.

An attempt to renegotiate the price and terms sometime during the due diligence period is a fairly common occurrence. Sometimes genuine problems are encountered and the deal needs to be restructured accordingly. Other times the buyer is just trying to squeeze down the price.

The real question the seller needs to address is, "How real is the problem and what is the likely affect on the future profits of the company?" Any experienced attorney or accountant can find "problems" or "new risks" which the buyer can use against the seller. However, it must be a significant problem before the seller agrees to reconsider the deal. If the problem is significant, one that will affect the projected future profits of the company by 10 percent or more, the deal should be renegotiated; if it is not significant, the existing agreement should stand. If the problem will have an effect on future profits of less than five percent the seller may want to take the position that it is not significant enough for a reduction in price. Thus there exists a grey area between 5 percent and 10 percent. The seller's decision on whether or not to renegotiate depends on the attractiveness of the offer and the seller's desire to close the deal.

Beware of cumulative problems. A buyer will sometimes present a number of small problems and then try to renegotiate on the argument that, although individually the problems are insignificant, when combined they become significant. Every business is subject to many different risks and potential problems—that is the nature of the beast. A seller cannot guarantee a specific level of future profits. The buyer must accept the inherent risks of the industry and marketplace.

Savvy buyers who are looking for a good deal will take advantage of every opportunity to negotiate a lower price. This is just one of the many aspects of the selling process. The seller should not be angry that the buyer tries to lower the price after an agreement has been reached. The seller just needs to be aware of the possibility of renegotiation and be prepared for it.

Chapter 20
The Close, Payoff, and Transition

The company has now been on the market for several months. The seller and advisors have expended countless hours of time. The sales literature about the company was prepared. The company's facility was made ready. Meetings were held with several interested buyers. Facility tours were conducted. Negotiation sessions went on for hours and hours. Offers to purchase were received from serious buyers. An offer was accepted and a letter of intent signed. Bankers became involved. The buyer's attorneys and advisors then spent weeks reexamining everything. More time was spent writing and negotiating the final sales documents. But now the time has come for the fruition of these efforts. It is time to close the deal. The business will be transferred to the buyer and the seller will receive payment.

Although most of the work has been done, it is not yet time to relax. A few things still need to be considered. The close is the final knot that will tie the package together. If this knot is not made properly, the entire package may come apart.

This chapter addresses items that are critical to closing. It will address the time period immediately following the close, the transition period when the reigns of management are transferred from the seller to the buyer.

THE CLOSE AND THE PAYOFF

The close is the meeting during which the ownership of the company is transferred to the buyer. The assets or stock of the company will be signed over to the new owner and payment will be made to the seller. The close is also a time for signing documents—both the buyer and seller will sign what seems like an endless number of papers. The sale contract, promissory notes, representations and warranties, noncompete agreements, and many other documents require signatures.

At the close, all of the legal requirements necessary to formalize the transaction are completed; everything is brought together in a formal and legal way. The close is the attorney's domain. The seller should rely on the attorney for guidance and to ensure that everything that is necessary is accomplished.

If possible, try to schedule the close so that it occurs in the morning. With a morning close there is time to solve any problems that may arise the same day. If necessary, any problems can be addressed immediately and the close can be completed in the afternoon.

It is also convenient to schedule the close to occur on one of the company's regular cutoff days, such as the first or last day of the month or the first or last day of the week. There are often adjustments made to the purchase price based upon inventory levels, accounts receivable balances, or some other item. By having the close on a normal cutoff day any amounts needed for adjustment are more readily available.

The close is not the time to review the final documents. The buyer and the buyer's attorney are present. There is also not enough time to review the documents thoroughly at the close. The seller should review the documents with the attorney and understand all of the documents before the close.

Due to the length and complexity of the documents, no one enjoys reviewing them. The temptation to rely on the attorney and not review them is great. The seller should avoid this temptation. It is the seller, not the attorney, that is signing the documents. The buyer will sue the seller not the attorney if something goes wrong with the transaction. The seller must take the time to review and understand all of the documents that are part of the final sales agreement.

SELLER'S REMORSE

Seller's remorse is an occurrence that happens more frequently than most people suspect. Quite simply, seller's remorse is the regret sellers feel as they begin to realize that the company will no longer belong to them. It is the doubt that creeps into seller's minds as they wonder if they are doing the right thing. Obviously, the closer to the finalization of the transaction, the more severe the seller's remorse becomes.

Unfortunately, seller's remorse occasionally results in the seller backing out of the transaction. The deal falls apart and the significant amount of time, money, and effort expended by both the buyer and the seller is wasted.

Seller's remorse is a very real emotional response to losing something of value. However, it is a terrible event when it destroys the transaction. If the seller properly considered his or her needs and understood the pros and cons of selling, then the decision to sell was the correct decision. If the seller begins to feel seller's remorse, he or she should review the notes that were made when the sale was first considered. Review the reasons for making the decision to sell. What were the needs that were considered? What were the seller's objectives in deciding to sell? A review of this data often brings the seller back to a more objective, less emotional frame of mind. The seller will realize that if the decision to sell was a good one when the selling process started, it will still be a good one when it is time for the close.

REPRESENTATIONS AND WARRANTIES

The phrase "representations and warranties" refers to a portion of the sales contract. In this section of the contract the seller represents that all of the information provided to the buyer is true and accurate and that no significant information about the company has been knowingly withheld. The seller also provides a warranty which stipulates that the seller will accept responsibility for anything related to the company that was misrepresented to the buyer.

The representations and warranties will cover any area of the company that the buyer feels is significant. There are many areas of a company's operations that are routinely addressed in the representations and warranties. The seller will represent that there are no debts or liabilities of the company other than those already identified. The seller will represent that the buyer has been made aware of any significant contingent liabilities of the company and that no additional significant contingent liabilities exist. The seller will also represent that the buyer has been made aware of any and all litigation in which the company is involved and that there is no other litigation. The seller will represent that the company has all of the permits and licenses necessary to operate; that all of those permits and licenses are transferable; and that they are being transferred to the buyer. The seller will represent that the company has no tax liabilities other than those identified. The seller will represent that the company is in compliance with all applicable laws and regulations.

The list of representations and warranties presented above is not complete. Each company is unique, and the buyer therefore may require a representation and warranty unique to the company or industry. What is important is that a seller understands what a representation and warranty is, and the liability the seller has as a result of that representation and warranty. Prior to the close, the seller and the seller's attorney need to discuss in detail all of the representations and warranties included in the sales contract.

INDEMNIFICATION CLAUSE

The indemnification clause is similar to the representations and warranties. It is a clause inserted into the contract to protect or indemnify the buyer against any unknowns. With this clause the seller accepts responsibility for any unknown liabilities, damages, or litigation that occur as a result of the operations of the company prior to the buyer purchasing the company.

An indemnification clause is included in nearly every sales contract. The seller's attorney will of course attempt to minimize the seller's liability. The seller and his or her attorney should review this clause in detail so that the seller understands the total extent of the potential liability.

THE OPINION LETTER FROM THE ATTORNEY

It is important that the seller's attorney provide the seller with a letter of legal opinion for the transaction. The letter should state that the sales transaction is legal, that all the applicable state and federal laws relating to the transaction have been complied with, and that the sales contracts are enforceable.

The purpose of this letter is twofold. First and most important is that it protects the seller. The seller has relied on the attorney in executing the sale. The attorney, by giving his or her legal opinion that the transaction has been executed properly, is accepting liability if anything is not legally correct and proper. Second, because of the potential liability, the attorney will be more thorough and exercise additional caution in protecting the seller's interests.

The seller should think of this letter as one of the things that must be done to insure that the seller's interests are properly looked after. The value of this letter in the long run may be immeasurable.

THE TRANSITION PERIOD

The transition period is the period during which the management of the company is transferred from the seller to the buyer. The actual ownership of the company is transferred at the close, but an effective transfer of management usually cannot be accomplished in one meeting. It often takes months of carefully planned effort to successfully transfer the skills and knowledge necessary to manage the business. During this time period both the buyer and seller are active in the operation of the company.

The steps required for an effective transition should be discussed and decided upon before the close. If it is decided that the seller is to remain with the company during the transition period, then an agreement specifying what is required from both parties should be made.

The agreement should determine the length of time the seller will remain, whether the seller will be active on a part-time or full-time basis, and what compensation, if any, the seller will receive.

When deciding these factors, both parties should consider what is reasonable as well as what they both want. Obviously, if the company is very complicated and the seller's presence is critical to its ongoing success, then the length of the transition will be long. If the business is not too complicated and the seller is not a critical part of day-to-day operations, then the transition period can be short.

The degree of involvement is also important. If the buyer is ready to step in as the manager and already has a good knowledge of the industry and the company, then the presence of the seller is not as important. Perhaps the seller can be available for two or three days a week in an advisory capacity on an as-needed basis. However, if the seller is needed to deal with clients or to assist in day-to-day management decisions, then his or her presence will be required on a full-time basis.

It is often expected that the seller will remain for a few weeks or a month to facilitate the transition. The assumption is also made that the seller will not receive any salary for this time. It is felt that the payment for the company includes the seller being available for a short period of time. This is a reasonable request by the buyer provided that the time period is truly short. If the seller is expected to be present for more than a few weeks, some type of compensation arrangement must be arranged. This arrangement should be formalized in a written agreement which is separate from the sales documents. This way, if something happens to prevent the seller from working for the buyer, it will not unravel the entire transaction.

The transition arrangement is extremely important. The success or failure of the transition period has a great impact on the future relations between the buyer and the seller. Make the effort to assure that a mutually agreeable arrangement is achieved.

Index